I0540243

Rebuilders
INTERNATIONAL, LLC

THE REBUILDERS
DIVORCE RECOVERY
WORKBOOK

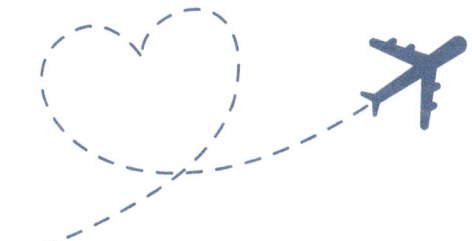

Essential Information and Exercises to help you Let Go and Move Forward

Release the anger sadness, end your loneliness, and start your new chapter

Why we created this workbook

Rebuilders International is committed to helping everyone suffering from heartbreak. We have been through this painful experience ourselves and we have tools and information that will ease the pain. We want to share this with everyone, regardless of location, finances, or schedule.

For this reason we offer a wide variety of videos, classes, coaching both live and recorded. The classes are offered both online and in-person, where available. These are available at Rebuilders.net

If you are struggling we are glad you are here. Before we jump in, here are a few resources to help you get started:

➤ We offer a **FREE divorce adjustment self test** at Rebuilders.net and also at our local in-person locations. It will give you an "emotional weather report" on how you are doing in 6 key areas. From there you can get suggestions and guidance on how specifically you can heal.

➤ We offer **weekly Support Groups**. Check Rebuilders.net for more information on times and how to sign up.

➤ **News and updates** are available through all social media channels (Facebook, Instagram, TikTok, X, and more).

A History of the Program

Dr. Bruce Fisher first began helping people deal with the emotional effects of the divorce in the 1970s. Ultimately he created a number of tools and information that we have built on and expanded . His work, more than 40 years ago, is still extraordinary and he paved the way in so many aspects of the divorce recovery process. He created the Fisher Divorce Adjustment Survey (the self test), the 19 Rebuilding Blocks, a curriculum for a 10-week divorce recovery group, and wrote the book Rebuilding When Your Relationship Ends.

It is estimated that over 1 million people have taken the program and more than 2.5 Million people have read his book. We are honored to continue the tradition and programs first created by Dr. Bruce Fisher.

TABLE OF CONTENTS

Divorce has been described as a "bomb going off in your life". It creates deep wounds. It affects every aspect of your life - your finances, your social status, your children and parents, and especially YOU. Here are some of the ways it most commonly affects people:

- Lose or gain weight rapidly.
- Difficulty sleeping
- Depression
- Job performance
- Parenting ability
- Intense grief and anger
- Difficulty focusing
- Loss of friends and family
- Questioning your purpose
- Loss of identity

You are not alone

What you are thinking, feeling, and dealing with is very common. 2.2 million people divorce in the US every year. Your circumstances are unique but the effects are common.

> "We must let go of the life we planned in order to embrace the life that is waiting for us."
> - Joseph Campbell

Things you can do today:

Take the Divorce Adjustment Self Test. Get an "emotional weather report" on how you are doing in 6 key areas. Then, get personalized suggestions and guidance based on your scores as to how to build a new life.

Ways to get more tools and information today:

- ☐ Divorce Adjustment Self Test: Rebuilders.net
- ☐ RB Podcast: Rebuilders.net/podcast
- ☐ RB Divorce Community Forum: Rebuilders.net/forum
- ☐ Rebuilders.net/free-divorce-support-resources
- ☐ RB Classes: Rebuilders.net/locations

Fill in your scores here:

Date of test: _____

Disentanglement _____

Grief _____

Anger _____

Self Worth _____

Social Self Worth _____

Social Trust _____

Overall Score _____

Journaling has scientifically been proven to help people process the intense stress of separation, divorce and heartbreak. We get stuck thinking the same things over and over again. We ask ourselves WHY and WHAT questions. It helps you to write these down, rather than letting your head spin over and over again, ruminating about the same things. Throughout this workbook there will be journal prompts. We encourage you to use these prompts or just journal to slow your mind and reflect.

Insider Tip:

Divorce is very isolating. You can turn to friends and family but often they don't have much to offer other than kindness and compassion. In this workbook we encourage you to move your thoughts and feelings from INSIDE of you to OUTSIDE of you. We will encourage you to do this by EXPRESSING them. Expressing is the art and science of moving something from being internal to being external. Writing in the journal pages is one of these ways that will help you move through your feelings and thoughts onto a page. Without expression, instead we DEpress, SUPpress, or REpress these thoughts and feelings.

Write your "story".

Write out what happened, how you felt, anything that is going through your head now. You will refer back to this throughout this workbook and it is helpful to start with "Here's where I am right now".

Your story (continued)

A Marriage Autopsy - The Death

When someone close to us passes away we tend to grieve publicly at a funeral with others. Divorce is different. There is no physical body and yet we feel an immense sense of loss. We are left to grieve alone.

So what has died in divorce? Our hopes and dreams for our future.

If the cause of death of the relationship isn't clear it is helpful to work through and process what happened. We can do this with stories or thoughts, or we can do it in a more thoughtful and considerate way. We will conduct an autopsy of the death of the relationship. By doing this we will begin to understand the cause of death, which may go very far back in time. For some people they saw red flags in the relationship before it even got serious. And yet they continued until those symptoms became a disease in the relationship.

Throughout this workbook you will have the opportunity to reflect on your relationship. You can process what happened and why in a way that helps you work through the cause of death and prevent future relationships from repeating the cycle.

> "By doing an autopsy, you take the mystery out of the train wreck." - Dr. Phil

Important Milestone	Details	Date
Time of Notification	The day you were told that the relationship was over or the day you told your partner that you were filing for divorce	
Time of Death	When was it really over (not time of notification)? This could have been days, weeks or even years before the words were actually spoken.	
Date Relationship Pronounced Dead	Final court date	

Reflections on the death of the marriage:

What did you learn about marriage from your parent's marriage or from another relative that may have contributed to the decline of the marriage?

Would you have liked to have had a marriage like your parents?

As you reflect on it, did you end up in a marriage like your parents? If so, in what ways?

What did you learn about marriage from the media that may have set up your relationship to fail?

The 3 Cs

People that are suddenly confronted with the reality of divorce often describe themselves as "lost" or a "mess".

They turn to one or more of the following

CONTENT	COMMUNITY	COACHING
Tools and Information:	**A Tribe**	**Trusted Expert**
Videos on: YouTube,	Friends and Family	Therapist
Vimeo, TikTok,	Support Group	Psychologist
Instagram,	Recovery Group	Coach
Podcasts	Church	Church Elder
Books	New relationship	

What we see is that they have a "go-to" path. They try lots of videos for example. They feel better, but they don't feel healed.

Some people will talk to their friends and family, or go to a support group at church. They feel better but not "recovered".

Others will seek out a therapist, a counselor or other trustworthy adviser. They will go for an hour a week for months or years. They will spend thousands of dollars and a lot of time. They TOO will feel better but most often not "recovered".

Many people seek one or two of these paths.

Tip:

Do all 3 together and you will heal faster.

Also, many people assume that this is just the way it is. That the wounds of divorce are permanent and something to get used to. Or subscribe to the old adage: "time heals all wounds"

Just doing one of the Cs results in limited healing. It is releasing a little bit of the pain, isolation, or confusion. People either give up or they get used to it and assume "this is just the way it is". After trying something they feel "good enough", accepting that they are scarred, and will just have to live with it. But life isn't meant to be lived just being "okay".

We see over and over again that you can heal those wounds, LET GO, and create a new future that is WAY better than you thought possible.

> "When you take the time it takes, it takes less time." - Julie T

Rick B's story: For 15 years after his divorce Rick hoped that his Ex would change her mind. That she would regret her decision. He waited, hoping for that day to come. When she remarried he still held out hope that she would come back. Sure enough, after a few years she got divorced. Did she come back to him? No. For 15 years He avoided confronting his own sadness and anger by focusing on the hope that she would come back. Finally, he decided to accept the reality that she wasn't coming back and that HE needed to heal.

Rick's story may sound extreme but it isn't. We have had people come to us more than 20 years after their divorce, finally realizing that they have wounds that they never healed.

> "Time doesn't heal all wounds. It scabs over them." - Nick Meima

If you face the pain you can heal it. If you avoid it or suppress it, then you are just putting it off for another day. Kind of like the dishes in the sink. You can deal with them today or tomorrow but they aren't going anywhere until you do something with them. You can heal from the pain and it doesn't have to take a long time.

We have found that if you do MORE than one "C" you will feel better and recover faster. If you do all 3 you will recover even faster, and with less cost (money and energy).

What have you tried so far?

What is working?

What isn't working?

What haven't you tried so far?

What are you going to try next?

The RIFT System

Heartbreak is an accurate image of what happens in divorce. There is a crack that forms in a relationship as it begins to unravel. This crack grows deeper and deeper until the marriage is irretrievably damaged.

A RIFT is a particular type of crack. It is not only deep but there is a shift or change in the relationship. It cannot simply be glued back together the way it was.

In our experience, the fastest healing occurs through a specific series of phases. We use a four-stage approach, called the "RIFT Recovery Model" to provide you with a clear roadmap to recovery. This process organizes various issues and offers a step-by-step guide based on proven tools and information. We will delve deeper into this in this workbook, with pages referencing the corresponding color and letter as needed. The word RIFT provides an easy to remember acronym to understand where you are in the process. Keep in mind that the recovery process is not perfectly sequential but there is a progression that we see people go through.

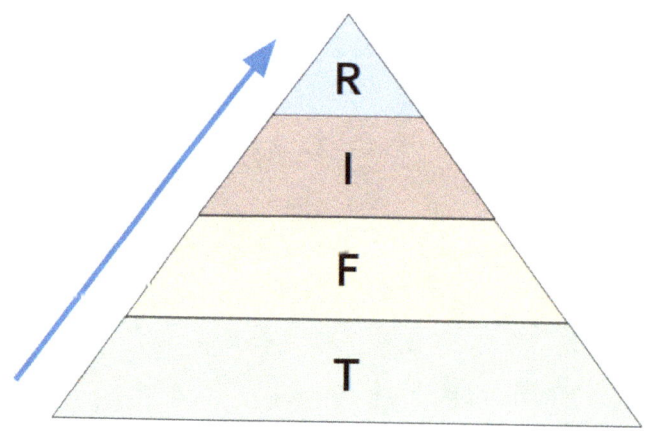

Figure 1. The RIFT Recovery Process

Briefly here are the four major stages:

T = THINKING

Starting at the bottom of the pyramid is the first step, your Thinking. If your mind is a mess it is hard to focus. Without sleep, without the ability to focus on the present, life is very difficult. So we start there.

F = FEELINGS

The "difficult" feelings - the ones we don't want to feel, are real. Many people are angry at their Ex but they don't want to be. They carry this anger with them. They don't think of themselves as an angry person but they can't seem to fully release it. These feelings must be expressed, that is they must move OUT of you. If not, they create mental, physical, social, and emotional issues that can destroy lives - yours and others around you.

The first two stages (T & F) are the "letting go" process. When you aren't thinking about the past nor carrying the intense feelings from everything that has happened then it is much easier to live in the present.

I = IDENTITY

A lot of people gave so much of themselves in their marriage. When their partner is no longer a major part of their lives they realize how much they lost themselves in it. Without them they are uncentered, uncertain.

This third stage builds on the previous stages. When you identify your thoughts and feelings, you can be more present to who you are. You can learn to be comfortable living alone in your own skin.

Many people make the mistake of moving on before they "Let Go". They prioritize building a new future, before processing the past. It is good to take care of yourself but not dealing with the past just carries it with you into your future. When they do this they find themselves trying to "run with a broken leg". Heal the wounds, then you can create a new future.

The first 3 steps are about looking inward. Getting to know yourself by investigating what is going on internally.

R = RELATIONSHIPS

We all need connection and intimacy. We need to be part of something bigger than ourselves. Some are satisfied with a healthy friend and family network. Others need more. Understanding how to have HEALTHY, fulfilling relationships is essential.

So how do you do it? When you build on the first three stages - when you are better able to understand your thoughts and feelings, when you know yourself as an individual, you are better able to give to others in a healthy way and to share who you really are. This is true intimacy and authenticity. When you can share yourself authentically, being vulnerable, showing that you care and that you are worthy of being loved, then you are better able to be in relationships that nurture and feed your soul.

You can use your self test scores to look at an "emotional weather report" for the 4 stages of the RIFT process:

Thinking - Look at your Disentanglement Score
Feelings - Look at your grief and anger scores
Identity - Look at your Self Worth and Social Self Worth Scores
Relationships - Look at your Social Trust Score

If your scores are 80 or less in any of the above areas, then focus on those phases, in the RIFT process (starting at your thinking).

Reflect on the RIFT process, how are you doing at each phase?

Community - The second "C"

People often seek out their friends and family as their primary love relationship collapses. Unfortunately our friends and family are rarely qualified or able to support them in all of the ways that they need. Here is a way to think about your relationships around you.

ROLODEX

In our lives we know a lot of people. When dealing with heartbreak we need support. Divorce results in shame, which causes people to isolate themselves. Yet when people reach out and connect with others going through divorce their recovery is faster. For many it actually strengthens relationships. When we reach out to others in times of our greatest need. However, it is easy to overwhelm our friends and family. Many people close to us want to give support but they don't know how or they simply can't absorb the weight of your emotions and ruminations. For this reason, it is helpful to consider HOW you can use people in your life most effectively. The ROLoDEX acronym can be used to assess where you need support. No one person can replace the loss of your significant other.

Respite: People that you can spend time with and help you NOT think about your divorce.

Opportunities: People in your life that you would like to grow or strengthen. Maybe people that you have lost touch with but you think could be improved.

Listeners: These are people that can listen without judgment. If you have a close friend you might say "I just need you to listen and hear me. I'll ask for advice if I need it -but right now I just want to share what is happening for me."

Doers: Some people show their love and support for you through actions or words. These are people that might help you move or sort through your Ex's stuff. They can mow your lawn while you meet with a lawyer.

Experts: Your Divorce coach, counselors, pastor, etc. These are people that are trained to help deal with heartbreak. Note that many therapists and counselors are trained to mend relationships. Rarely are they trained to help you heal from the ending of a relationship. Choose carefully.

X: Cross them off your list (for now). Some people draw energy away from you. Maybe they want to be helpful but they aren't. Sometimes parents, siblings and friends are not helpful. It is okay to say "I really don't want to talk about my divorce right now. I am struggling, but just being able to spend some time with you is what I need. I'm getting some help from a divorce specialist, and that is making a big difference.."

Name of Support Person	Circle how they can support you (or not)
	R O L D E X
	R O L D E X
	R O L D E X
	R O L D E X
	R O L D E X
	R O L D E X
	R O L D E X
	R O L D E X
	R O L D E X
	R O L D E X
	R O L D E X
	R O L D E X
	R O L D E X
	R O L D E X
	R O L D E X
	R O L D E X

Support Groups vs Recovery Groups

Many people seek support groups. They are really good if you know what you are getting into. A support group is designed to give you support and community. It is designed to provide a safe space to be with others during one of the most difficult times in life. However, many people come to support groups wanting to heal. That isn't the purpose of a support group. A recovery group is specifically focused on results, feeling not just better but significantly better. It is for people that want to learn and grow from their breakup.

Characteristic	Most Support Groups	Recovery Groups
Size of Group	Large Group	Small Group
Content Strategy	No plan	Structured growth
Facilitator Training	Volunteer	Trained Expert
Dating and hookups	Allowed	Not Allowed
Duration of group	Indefinite	Specific (10-weeks)
Focus of group	Be around others	Results through healing

What you can do today to have a support system:

- Join a **Facebook Group.** There are a lot of online forums where you can ask questions and have others to share your situation with.
- Create an account on **MeetUp.com** and find groups that interest you. We run a number of Support Groups on Meetup but you should also look for other groups that have nothing to do with support. Meeting others with similar interests will help you feel "normal".
- Create an account on **Reddit** (you can interact anonymously) and join the divorce group. It's massive.
- Join a **Rebuilders 10-Week program (a Recovery group)**

What will you do to grow your support and recovery network?

Coaching - The Third "C"

The last strategy that people pursue is to find a trusted professional. Someone that has training. Someone that can guide them out of this difficult time in their life. Often people turn to:

- ☐ Therapists
- ☐ Psychologists
- ☐ Counselors
- ☐ Coaches
- ☐ Religious leaders (minister, pastor, etc)

These people have shown an interest in helping others. They have invested in themselves in order to guide others. There is a wide variety in divorce experts. If you are seeing the same couples therapist or counselor that tried to keep you together they likely are not trained in how to let go of a relationship and recover. You would not see your cardiologist for a broken arm. Why see the same person that tried to keep you together to help you move on with your life?

Here are some criteria when choosing a divorce guide:

- Have they been divorced? Do NOT work with someone that hasn't been divorced and hasn't processed it for themselves.
- Is there a structured plan? (many people sign up for therapy sessions and it becomes crisis management - instead of systematically working through the issues)
- Are they able to handle the wide range of issues that come with divorce? (Some focus on one particular model to solve a wide range of issues)
- What is their training? (A life coach is not qualified for the depth and range of trauma caused by divorce. They should at least have 2-3 years of training applicable to divorce and issues related to divorce).
- What can they guarantee? (Most experts only promise to help you. They can't tell you how long it will take. What if you don't feel like you got your money's worth after 3 months? Rebuilders has a guarantee)

The Obstacle is the way

The concept of "the obstacle is the way" is based on the idea that life's difficulties can be used as learning experiences to help us grow and become stronger. It's a reminder that instead of looking at obstacles as something to avoid, we should view them as an opportunity to better ourselves. By facing our struggles head-on, we can develop a more resilient mindset and become better prepared for anything life throws our way. Ryan Holliday's book on this exact topic is fascinating and highly recommended.

You are going to resist doing certain activities in this book. The pages in this workbook are based on proven tools and information. When you find yourself thinking "I don't want to do that" remember the phrase by Marcus Aurelius:

> **"The impediment to action advances action.**
> **What stands in the way becomes the way."**

What obstacles do you have in your life?

What obstacles are you going to turn towards instead of away from today? Explain

The Change Model

So if we know that "The Obstacle is the Way" then why doesn't everyone do what we know is good for us(such as exercise)? We have a useful equation that can help you understand change and how to create change in your life. We call the following equation the "change model".

$$C=D+V+F>R$$

C = Change
D = Dissatisfaction with how things are now
V = Vision of what is possible
F = First concrete steps that can be taken toward the vision.
R = Resistance

If the product of these factors is greater than R (resistance) then change is possible.

The bigger you change, the more you are going to grow. The bigger the commitment, the bigger the payoff. In other words, where there's no risk, there is no reward.

What do you want to change in your life?

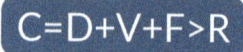

What are you dissatisfied with?

How much dissatisfaction do you have? Explain the impacts on your life. Be as detailed as possible.

What is your Vision?

What steps can you take TODAY to fulfill your vision? (Break big steps down into small steps. Focus on the first step that you can accomplish by tomorrow.)

The MORE Motivational Exercise

What is your goal?

M = What is your motivation? What is your "why"? (Why do you want to do this? If you complete it, what will it get you?)

O = What obstacles are you going to encounter? Time? Fear?

R = Resources - what do you have that you can use to help you accomplish your goals?

E = Execution - How exactly are you going to do to achieve that goal?

Research shows that the more specific you are the more you accomplish your goals. What days and times will you work on your divorce recovery? Be realistic about when you will work on this. In the left column write the action. Under the days, write in what time you will accomplish them.

Actions	Mon	Tues	Wed	Thurs	Fri	Sat	Sun

Sometimes it is overwhelming to do this on your own. If you need help you can sign up for coaching sessions with a Rebuilders Divorce Coach.

Obstacles to Letting Go

Don't get stuck before you even start. Here are some things to focus on first.

Denial | "Denial is the shock absorber for reality."

When you find yourself saying "I can't believe this is happening", "I can't believe he/she is doing that", "He/she doesn't really want a divorce". These are all versions of denial - not accepting the reality of your situation.

DENIAL IS NORMAL.

It is okay to struggle to adjust to your new reality. However, when you keep saying things that deny this new life to yourself you are avoiding reality.

Arguing with reality is not healthy in the long term.

If you find yourself in denial:

1. Acknowledge the situation and its impact on you.
2. Identify any underlying feelings of sadness, guilt, or anger that might be causing the denial.
3. Accept that the denial is there and talk about it openly.
4. Tell yourself "This is my new life" or "He/she is a different person now and not a part of my life like before."
5. Develop a plan for moving forward in a constructive manner instead of denying the situation.
6. Make a conscious effort not to push aside difficult topics but rather face them head on and process them as they come up in conversations or situations.

Arc you in Denial? If so, how will you come to accept your new reality?

Fear

Fear is an emotion triggered by a perceived threat. It usually produces physiological responses, such as increased heart rate, sweating and shaking. Fear can be both beneficial and detrimental; it can motivate us to take action or make us freeze in our tracks. It is one of the most basic and primal human emotions, felt in all cultures across humanity.

Fear in divorce is often because people are facing a dramatically different future that doesn't seem as safe and stable as what they had planned.

FEAR = False Expectations Appearing Real

If you feel a lot of fear, know that it is normal. Give yourself credit for paying attention to your fear. If you let it overcome you and disable you it can be debilitating. So here are some tips for overcoming fear:

Identify the source of your fear and acknowledge it. What are you afraid of?

Challenge negative thoughts or beliefs about the situation. What is UNLIKELY to happen?

Focus on positive thinking by noting the possible outcomes and imagining success instead of failure. What is LIKELY to happen?

Create action. Do something that gets you moving forward. Even small steps can feel good when you are affected by fear. Some ideas:

- Listen to music that motivates you
- Call a friend and ask for encouragement.
- Write a phrase or quote on a piece of paper that inspires you.
- Read "Man's Search for Meaning" by Viktor Frankl.
- Watch Tim Ferris's Ted Talk on Fear.
- Practice mindful breathing techniques such as deep breaths, counting to ten, or picturing a calming environment.

What ACTION are you going to take?

What do I fear?

Define Write down the worst case scenarios	Prevent What can you do to prevent each of these scenarios from happening, even a little bit.	Repair What could you do to repair the damage if it does happen, even a little bit?

What might be the benefits of an attempt or partial success?

What is the Cost of Inaction? (Emotionally, physically, financially, etc.)

In 6 months:

In 1 year:

In 3 years:

Initiators - Guilt

If you were the one that decided to end the marriage you are the "Initiator". Often the Initiator feels guilty, even if the marriage was abusive or unhealthy.

Feeling guilty can occur as a result of various factors, such as having done something wrong or feeling responsible for something that has gone wrong. Guilt may also be a sign of being trapped in a thought pattern that prevents you from taking action and moving on. To tackle this, it is important to acknowledge the feeling and talk to someone about it or join a group, if necessary. Additionally, try to replace negative thoughts with more positive ones and look at how you can make things better in the future rather than focusing on the past.

Christianity teaches:

> Love thy neighbor as thyself

While most people agree with this, we often see that they misinterpret it as:

> **Love thy neighbor BEFORE thyself**

This is wrong. <u>You must put yourself first THEN love the others around you</u>. Giving all of yourself to others without taking care of you isn't love, it is martyrdom.

If you are the Initiator:

Do you feel guilty?

Did you tolerate behaviors that you shouldn't have?

Resisters - Rejection

When your spouse makes the decision to end the marriage it can be very painful. You are the "Resister" - the one that didn't want the divorce. You can fight it but often it is too late. When one person decides to leave the trust and communication are gone. For the Resister, feelings of anger and grief are often MUCH more intense than for the Initiator. The reason is that the Initiator often has been experiencing grief and anger often for years before making the decision to end the marriage. The Resister is often unaware of how "bad" the situation is. The feelings of Rejection are very common. Some people also feel betrayed by their Ex.

It can be difficult to cope with the feeling of rejection. Here are some suggestions for dealing with it:

- Acknowledge your feelings and allow yourself to experience them without judgment.
- Look at the facts and not your thoughts or beliefs.
- Connect with people who make you feel good and accepted, such as family and friends.
- Make a plan to overcome your feeling of rejection by deciding to make a positive change in your life or seeking professional guidance.
- Focus on things that you can control and take action accordingly, one step at a time, rather than letting fear lead you down an uncertain path.

> "The best revenge is deciding to be happy."

If you are the Resister:

Do you feel rejected?

Did you give the best version of yourself in the relationship? Explain

Blame

Blame is directing the pain you feel inside at your Ex. It is tempting to blame your ex but it takes away your power, and more often than not, it isn't productive in helping you move on. Instead, focus on accepting what has happened, taking responsibility for how you responded, and healing the hurt inside.

> **"It's better to feel pain, than nothing at all. The opposite of love is indifference." -The Lumineers: Stubborn Love**

If you are hurting, it means that you loved your partner. You invested in them. If you didn't feel anything then it wasn't really a marriage of love.

Do you blame your partner for the breakup? Explain

Do you blame yourself for the breakup? Explain

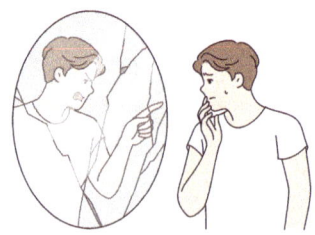

Self-Limiting beliefs

> "**Whether you think you can or you can't, you are right.**" - Henry Ford

We all have that voice inside that isn't nice. When you say the same thoughts to yourself over and over they become beliefs. You then find evidence that those thoughts are true. **Circle at least 10 self limiting beliefs that resonate with you.** Add your own if you don't see them here.

- I am a failure
- I can't make things happen
- I don't deserve a better life
- Things just don't work out for me.
- It's all my parents' fault.
- People look right through me
- That's just my luck!
- I will never find love.
- I am not worthy of being loved.
- All the good ones are taken
- I am useless on my own.
- I need someone to take care of me.
- My relationships just never work out
- I am too old
- I am not smart enough
- I am afraid to fail
- I am not attractive enough
- I am a terrible cook
- I don't make enough money
- I suck at technology
- No one wants me.
- Why am I so bad at this?
- I am not enough on my own
- Others are just going to step on my toes

- I need someone to complete me.
- Love never works out for me.
- I always get hurt (or dumped, or betrayed).
- You just can't trust anybody in a relationship
- Why don't I know how to make it work?
- I need someone in my life at all times.
- Putting yourself out there only results in getting hurt.
- I need to be someone else other than myself for others to like me.
- There just isn't somebody out there for me.
- I need somebody else in my life to make me feel useful
- My family is always trying to keep me down
- Doing something besides what my family wants is betraying them.
- I can't do what my family doesn't want me to do.
- I just have to put up with what I don't like.
- I have to do what my parents say or else (even as a grown-up).
- Others are going to hate me if I stand up for myself.

Add your own self limiting beliefs

A growth mindset

A growth mindset is the belief that one can develop their abilities, skills and knowledge over time. It is based on the idea that intelligence and talent are not fixed, but rather can be developed through effort and dedication. A growth mindset encourages individuals to embrace challenges as opportunities for personal growth, take risks and view mistakes as learning experiences.

Use a growth mindset to SHIFT your beliefs. Some examples are:

"It's ok to make mistakes and learn from them."
"I can always grow and learn new skills."
"I am open to feedback and see it as a way to improve."
"My effort will determine my success, not my talent."
"I view challenges as opportunities for growth."
"I believe I can achieve anything I set my mind to."
"My resilience will help me overcome obstacles."
"Making mistakes helps me become better and stronger."
"Taking risks is how I become more confident in myself."
"If I fail, I will use it as an opportunity for learning and growth."

One of the most powerful, honest things you can say has to do with creating a new image of yourself. You say it this way:

- "I'm the kind of person who....."
    - Exercises regularly
    - Takes care of myself
    - Loves myself and others with compassion
    - Cherishes the good in myself and others.

Write who you ARE as if it has already happened:

I'm the kind of person who

Describe in detail, the best version of you. The one that is everything you have imagined that you will be. Don't let your self-judgment stop you. Play, have fun with this. Who could you be if there were no constraints? Think of everything (physically, emotionally, support network, financially, how you spend your time, etc).

The Trauma Tree

Circle your trauma roots and fruits

Circle your healthy roots and fruits

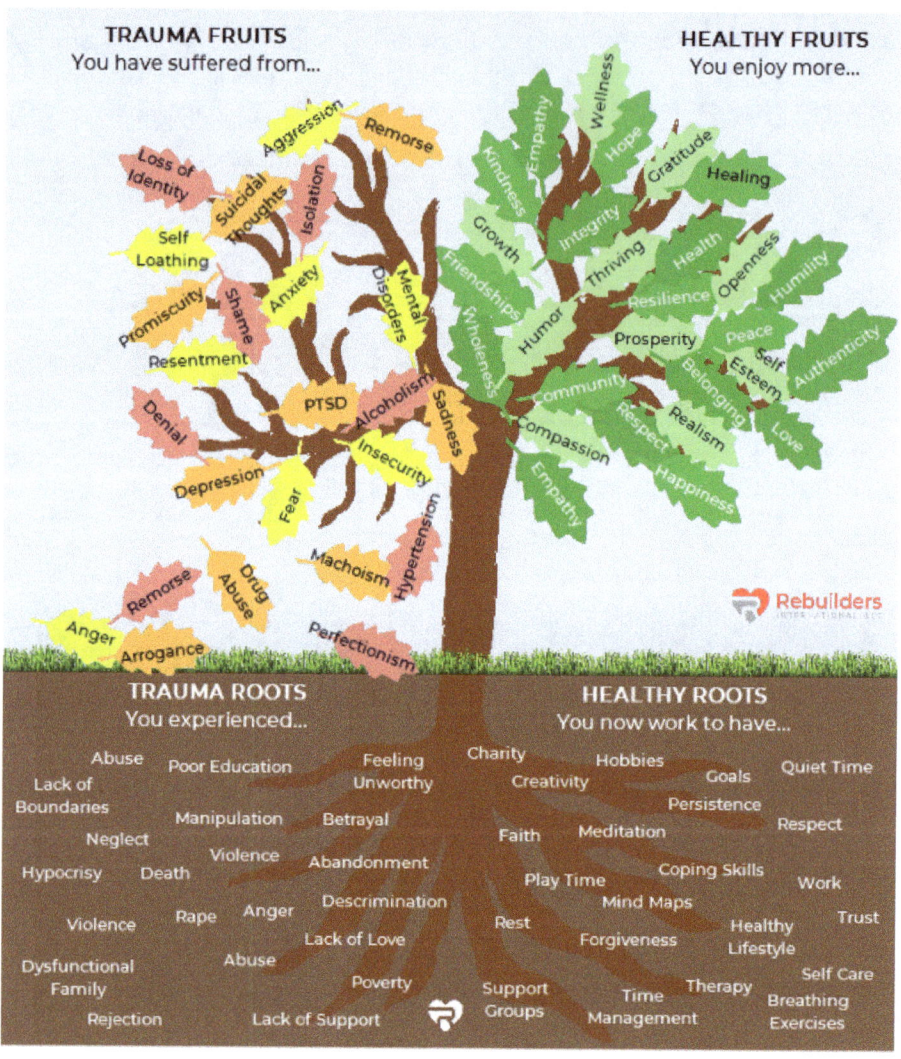

What trauma leaves are present in your life due to unaddressed traumatic roots (Circle them)?

What will you do to turn your roots and fruit from traumatic into healthy?

The Unanswerable Questions

It is common for people to get stuck in a loop of asking themselves the same questions over and over again. Which of these questions do you find yourself saying to yourself over and over again?

- What happened?
- Why?
- What could I have done differently?
- What was my role?
- What was my Ex's role?
- Should I have ever married?
- Should I have seen this earlier?
- How could he/she suddenly be behaving this way?
- _____
- _____

These questions are "unanswerable" in that even if you have the answers (and you may know them) you keep asking them. WHY?! Why do you keep going over them again and again?

It has to do with your thinking. You are trying to process the pain. You have moved past the Obstacles for Letting Go but you aren't sure what to do with it.

For now, just be aware of the questions you are asking yourself. As you go through this workbook you will see that you will begin asking them less and less.

Your Disentanglement Score

My Disentanglement score _____ (from the self test).

Disentanglement has to do with how much you are still thinking about your Ex and the past.

The Prison Cell of Not-Enoughness

When you were born, you were completely dependent on your parents and others to take care of you. At around age 5 you start to be able to be somewhat independent. Yet what comes with this stage is a thought that "I am not safe." In fact, we make the mistake of thinking that there must be something wrong with me. At that young age we take it a step further: "there is something wrong with me. " As you age, without lots of love and support you begin to believe it. You get proof in many ways. The thoughts become beliefs and they become "true".

So as a strategy to deal with the belief that there is something wrong with me, we develop strategies to compensate because we also mistakenly believe that other people are "okay". So shame grows and we do more and more to make up for it.

We call this the "Prison cell of not-enoughness".

At the root of the prison cell is the belief that "I am not enough". And on the ceiling is written the words "I'm all alone". On the walls people write additional thoughts like "I'm unlovable." "I'm not smart enough." "I can't handle it" "I need help"

What did you tell yourself when you were young?

(Un) Consciousness

When we are young, our brains are constantly absorbing and processing new information about the world around us. We learn how to interact with people, form relationships and take care of ourselves in order to stay safe from harm. All of this learning contributes to the formation of our beliefs and values, which can shape the choices we make in life.

It is said that an average person has between 50,000 and 70,000 thoughts a day, many of which are repetitive and stem from previous experiences or learned behavior. Our conscious minds would have difficulty processing all of this information, so most decisions and thoughts are pushed to the unconscious mind. This is like a vast repository of information that can affect our behavior and decision-making without us even being aware of it.

Learning to stop and question some of our basic beliefs can change our outlook and understanding of our worlds. In the "Prison cell of not enoughness" you explored some of your fundamental beliefs.

We are going to re-examine some of those beliefs and see how they influence you and your relationships with others.

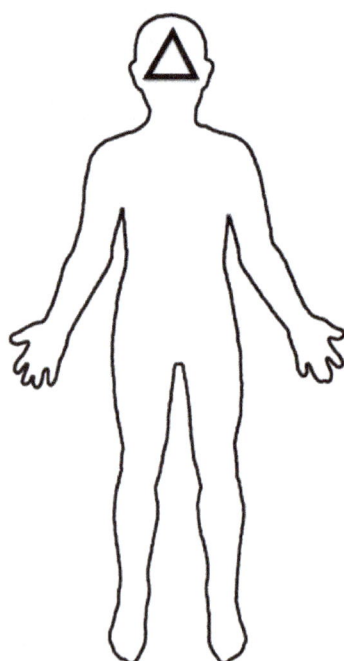

The Drama Triangle

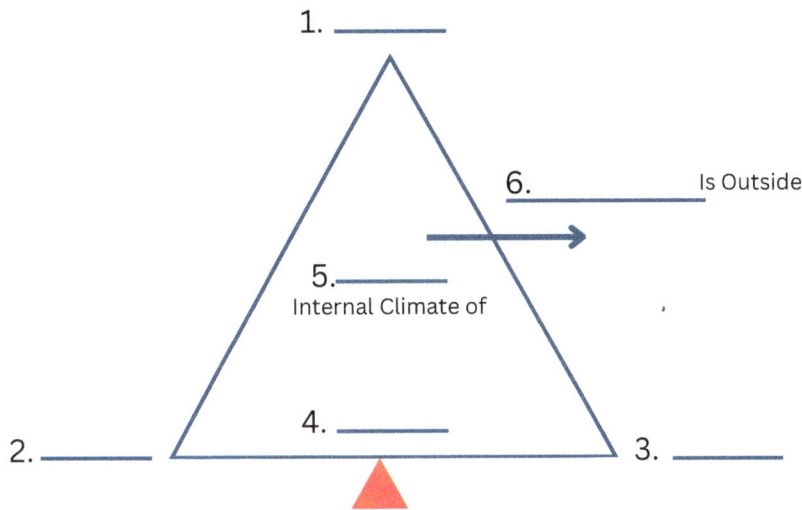

1. _____

6. _____ Is Outside

5. _____
Internal Climate of

4. _____

2. _____

3. _____

Belief is that I _____ which leads to the misuse of _____ = _____

Behaviors that indicate Victim Consciousness

_____

_____

_____

_____

Reacting vs _____

There is a mentality of:

_____

_____

_____

Find the answers on the following pages

The Drama Triangle was first developed by Stephen Karpman. Rebuilders has found that it is an excellent foundation for understanding ourselves and our relationships with others. We have expanded the concept of the Drama Triangle to include something we call Victim Consciousness. We will explore this more later.

To start, the three points on the triangle are Roles (1), Victim (2), and Persecutor (3). Each role is filled by a person in any given situation or relationship. Most people have a default "starting position" on the triangle.

A Victim is someone who believes that they have no power or control over the situation and often looks to others for help or support.

A Persecutor is someone who blames and criticizes the victim or rescuer for their problems.

Roles are behaviors that we identify with to save the victim or protect against a persecutor. We will discuss this more when we get to Maladaptive Behaviors.

When a person is living in Victim Consciousness there is no Sense of Self (4). We don't know who we are because we are defined by what is happening outside of us.

The most important of all concepts is that at the center of Victim Consciousness (5) is that "I AM NOT ENOUGH" or some version of this. We believe that we are defective, broken, unequal or unqualified. There is something wrong with us. This is the most powerful concept and when you really understand it and absorb it you will see how this secret belief influences every other part of our lives. Another way to say this is that we have "Self Limiting Beliefs" that think are true (see page 29) for examples.

When you think that you are not enough there is an internal climate of:

Shame	Anxiety
Fear	Guilt
Inadequacy	Depression
Numbing	Desperation
Blame	Resentment

When we have any of the characteristics listed above the Power is OUTSIDE (6) of us. We have no control, no agency in our life.

Other ways of know that you are living in the Drama Triangle:
You REACT instead of RESPONDING to situations around us.

When you REACT you exhibit one or more of the following:

Are defensive	Withdraw
Submit	Feel aggressive
Rationalize	Deflect
Blame	Defend

You operate in a mentality of

- [ ] Black or White
- [ ] Either/Or
- [ ] Right OR Wrong
- [ ] Good OR Bad

We call this way of being: "Victim Consciousness"

It is a consciousness, a way of living our lives, without realizing the impact it has on us. 90% of relationships are based on one or more people operating in Victim Consciousness.

> "Suffering is universal. But victimhood is optional. We don't get to choose what happens to us, but we do get to choose how we respond to our experience." - Edith Eger

Can you see yourself in Victim Consciousness?

If so, reflect on what you have learned as you become aware of this "way of being" and how it has influenced your life. If not, can you see that your Ex is in Victim Consciousness?

Codependency

Codependency is a pattern of behavior in which one or both people depend heavily on the other for emotional or psychological support. The codependent person relies on the other person to satisfy their needs, while neglecting their own sense of identity and health.

Modern society teaches us that codependency is normal and healthy. It's not!

> **"You complete me!" Jerry Maguire (UGH)**

When we marry people typically think a healthy relationship is:

"My job is to make you happy, and your job is to make me happy."

"I'll be okay if you are okay, and if you are not okay then I'm not okay."

And when one person isn't happy, they blame the other person for it.

The reality is that we go through life, living in Victim Consciousness, looking for happiness "somewhere". If we have the right job, enough money, live in a big house, travel a lot, marry the right person, etc THEN we will be happy. Eventually life happens and we realize that these things we have been working for, for so long, don't make us happy. Neither does our spouse.

Learning how to NOT be in a codependent relationship means taking responsibility for your own happiness. You are:
- Your thoughts
- Your feelings
- Your beliefs
- Your behaviors

Being able to be in a healthy relationship means being healthy yourself. It means NOT living in the Drama Triangle. So how do you do that? Ah, read on!

Think about your current or past relationships. In what ways have you relied on your partner to meet your emotional and psychological needs?
How has this reliance impacted your sense of self and your overall well-being?

Consider times when you have felt unhappy or dissatisfied in your relationship. How often did you find yourself blaming your partner for your unhappiness? Reflect on what underlying beliefs or expectations contributed to this pattern of thinking.

List three ways in which you can take responsibility for your own happiness without depending on a partner. How can you nurture your thoughts, feelings, beliefs, and behaviors to cultivate a healthy sense of self and well-being?

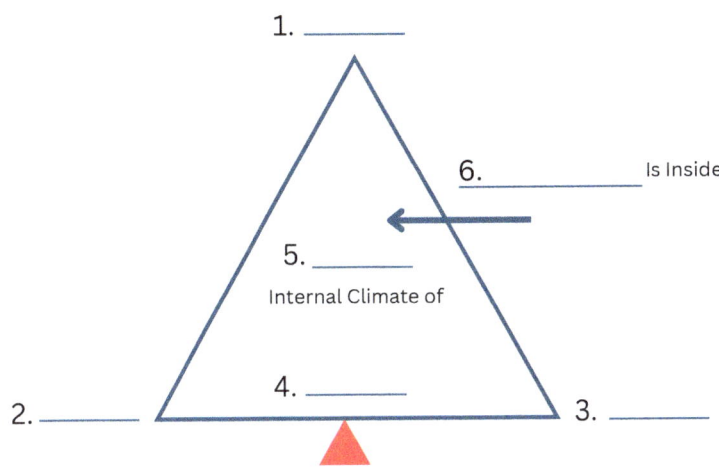

Observer Consciousness

The Empowerment Triangle

1. _____

6. _____ Is Inside

5. _____
Internal Climate of

4. _____

2. _____

3. _____

Behaviors that indicate Observer Consciousness

_____

_____

_____

_____

Responsive vs _____

There is a mentality of:

_____

_____

_____

> "The world as we have created it is a process of our thinking. It cannot be changed without changing our thinking." - Albert Einstein

> "When we are no longer able to change a situation, we are challenged to change ourselves." - Viktor Frankl

The Empowerment Triangle is a different way of BEING. When a person is living inside the Empowerment Triangle there are three characteristics that are working TOGETHER, instead of being in one corner or the other (like in the Drama Triangle). These three characteristics are:

- ☐ Caring (1)
- ☐ Vulnerability (2)
- ☐ Assertiveness (3)

At the center of this way of living is knowing (5):

"I AM ENOUGH"

Some other versions of this are:
- I am a beautiful person
- I am a gem
- I am the son or daughter of God (if you believe in God)

The power is INSIDE you (6). This doesn't mean you are an island and can do everything alone. But you know who you are and who you aren't. You care about people but don't care what they think. You place higher value on what YOU think about yourself.

There is a sense of self (4). You build your own self-esteem. You are guided by your own values and beliefs that are based on striving toward something that inspires, not away from something you fear.

There is an internal climate of ALIVENESS!

People living in the Authentic Triangle carry the Power of Love with them wherever they go. They are constructive. They respect everyone, regardless of who they are and their behaviors. They are compassionate with themself and others. They value well-being, in themselves and others. They have a belief in self-responsibility and they live it. They allow for more than one viewpoint

They live in a world that allows for "BOTH" or "AND" to exist.
They are responsive rather than reactive.
They are accepting of where others are in their life without feeling the need to change/fix them.

Reflect on your life. Can you see times in your life that you were living in Observer Consciousness?
If so, what was it like for you? What was happening in your life that contributed to your "aliveness"?

The Work

In this section we build on the incredible collection of information created by Byron Katie. You can find more at: http://www.everypathis.org/ . We also highly recommend her book "Loving What Is".

Byron Katie created a process she calls "The Work". It can be very helpful when you have thoughts that you keep thinking that create suffering.

For example, "I can't trust (wo)men". It is a simple thought and one that we hear often from people that have dealt with infidelity or have gone through a high conflict divorce. It is an obvious choice, as a way to protect ourselves.

One of the most powerful things that Katie teaches is that:

our thoughts create our suffering.

For example, Byron makes the statement "We really believe that we need other people to change in order for us to be happy. That's insane. "

We love the concepts she teaches because it gives us tools to investigate our thoughts in a non-threatening way. We often have thoughts that we don't question or observe, we just assume that they are true and they are the only option. Byron Katie slows down the automated thinking and creates "An Inquiry" into these thoughts that cause our suffering.

An inquiry can change your life.
So let's get started.

There are some basic ground rules for this investigation into your thoughts:

1. Don't argue with reality. Often we find ourselves wanting to justify, rationalize, or defend thoughts that, once examined closely, don't make sense.

2. Stay focused on YOU. It is easy to want to change others, or get them to understand something. This is impossible. Stay with what is going on inside of you and stick to what you can control - primarily your thoughts, your behaviors, your beliefs. Otherwise you start trying to control other people's thoughts, behaviors, beliefs, and even what they say.

3. You cannot stop thinking. Thoughts will come and go. It is our attachment to thoughts that create our suffering. You are not your thoughts.

4. We create our history and stories based on our thoughts. These stories can be about the past, the future, and the present. Remember that every thought is objective.

"Don't believe everything you think."

5. There is no RIGHT or wrong answer. It is an investigation into our thoughts in a structured way. You can agree or disagree. Instead, pay attention to your own resistance. When you feel resistance, try to become curious. Why do I resist that?

Think of a situation in your marriage or divorce that bothers you or you keep saying to yourself over and over again. Try to use simple, short sentences as you write this down:

Frameworks for your situation that you can use (fill in the information):

I am _____ with _____ because _____
         (emotion)   (name)

I want _____ to _____
       (name)

_____ should/shouldn't _____
   (name)

I need _____ to _____ in order for me to be happy.
      (name)

The Work Flowchart

Based on The Work by Byron Katie

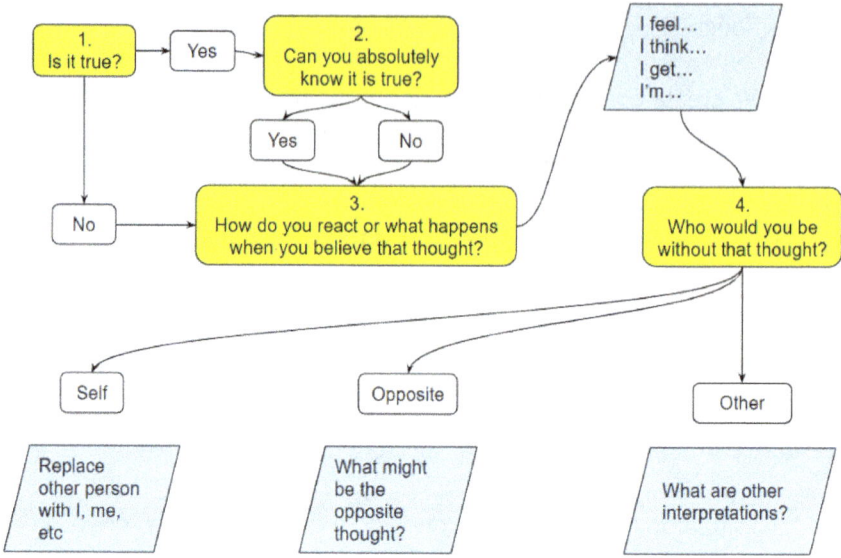

Take ONE of the statements you completed previously and answer the following questions:

1. Is it true? (circle one) Yes No

2. Can you ABSOLUTELY know it is true? (circle one)   Yes No

3. How do you react or what happens when you believe that thought? Here's a hint, before you have that thought, how do you feel? THEN when you have the thought we are investigating, what changes in your mood, feelings, thoughts, behaviors, etc?

        a. I feel _____
        b. I think _____
        c. I get _____
        d. I'm _____

4. Now who would you be if you didn't have that thought? (More alive, kinder, loving, happy, etc). Another way of thinking about this is, "If I let this thought go, would it be helpful to me?" or "Is it worth keeping my attachment to that thought?"

The Turnarounds

Now the next step in the process is to take the painful thought and look at it in different ways.

Self Turnarounds:

Take your original statement and replace the Other person name with I, me, myself, etc. For example:
I am angry with Bill because he had an affair.
→ I am angry with myself because he had an affair.

You can play with replacing the statements to have them make sense. After you change the original statement, ask yourself:
Is that true or truer than the original statement?

Maybe the thoughts of him having an affair are making you feel unloved or unattractive?

Write out your SELF turnaround by rewriting your original statement:

Opposite Turnarounds

Take your original statement and reverse the statement and see what comes up for you:
For example:
Bill shouldn't have had an affair. → Bill should have had an affair.

After you change the original statement, ask yourself:
Is that true or truer than the original statement?
Maybe it is a good thing that Bill had an affair because it allowed you to see how unhealthy the marriage is that he would do that. Maybe the affair is the red flag you needed to see in order to make a change?

Write out an Opposite Turnaround for your original statement:

Other Turnarounds

Sometimes simply looking at the original statement and asking yourself "What might some other possible interpretations be?" Remember, they don't have to be true, but they could be. You are simply looking at how the thoughts you have create your suffering.

What are some Other Turnarounds that might be possible?

In Summary:

The Work by Byron Katie is very powerful and can help you shift out of painful thoughts that are difficult to let go of. What it fails to do is address FEELINGS. It is highly focused on logic. We know that people are very good at thinking their way out of their feelings by suppressing, repressing and depressing them. Anger is a feeling that can't be rationalized. It must be felt and EXPRESSED in a healthy way. Nevertheless, using The Work in combination with other tools in this workbook can be transformational.

(Mal) Adaptive Behaviors

This chart on the left shows a continuum of maladaptive/survivor behaviors. Identify those maladaptive behaviors of your mother (M), father (F), former love partner (E), and yourself (Y). Each of these maladaptive behaviors will limit your ability to get your Real needs met (to be explained later). Often these behaviors were based on self limiting beliefs. Also, these come from the Roles you play in the Drama Triangle.

	Maladaptive	M	F	E	Y
Perfectionist	Expects perfection in others				
	Provides rigid limits to others				
	Wants to look good				
	Strives for perfection				
	Can elicit defensive response in others				
	Makes others feel not ok				
	Wants to change another				
	Never enough				
Over-responsible	Smothering behavior				
	Gives another a fish				
	Giving is self-serving				
	Triggers adaptive response in others				
	Controlling				
	Caretaker				
	Enabler				
	Feels selfish when taking care of self				
Rational-logical	Rigid				
	Unable to access feelings				
	Uses only facts and interpretations				
	Dictator				
	Uses learned survival strategies				
	Concerned with doing it the right way				
	Expresses opinions, tries to convince others				
Rebel	Wants own way				
	Upsets system				
	Behavior results in more chaos				
	Concerned with rebelling				
	Selfish manipulation				
	Elicits criticism from others				
Needy & Hurt child	Mimics others				
	Pretends to have a good time				
	Expresses what others feel and express				
	Concerned about fitting in				
	Follower				
	Elicits "rescuing" from others				

Authentic	
Gives constructive feedback to others	Strives for excellence
Provides healthy limits to others	
Not concerned with appearances	
Strives for excellence	
Elicits appropriate response in others	
Helps others to feel ok	
Accepts others	
Satisfied with accomplishments	
Empathetic nurturing	Responsible to self
Teaches another to fish	
Giving is unselfish	
Elicits natural response in others	
A catalyst to another's growth	
Caregiver	
Tough love	
Is able to do self-care	
Flexible	Thoughts & Feelings balanced
Able to access feelings	
Uses all sub-personality parts	
Chairman of the Board	
Makes loving choices	
Concerned about others	
Expresses beliefs and listens to others	
Able to bring about change	Healthy identity
Helps system work better	
Behavior results efficiency/effectiveness	
Adjusts to situation	
Transparency	
Elicits support in others	
Creative and spontaneous	Natural & creative child
Fun loving	
Expresses feelings easily	
Inner directed	
Leader	
Elicits spontaneity in others	

Marriage Autopsy - The Cause

Earlier in life when most people marry, we choose a person to spend our life with. We have certain reasons for "why this person". Certainly we usually like or love that person. But for many there are other factors as to why we choose that person. **Select one or more of the reasons you committed yourself to this other person:**

- [ ] Fell in love
- [ ] An affair
- [ ] Uncomfortable being single or alone
- [ ] I was lonely
- [ ] He/she was attractive
- [ ] Wanted to get out of my parents' house
- [ ] Because marriage is expected
- [ ] Wanted someone to take care of
- [ ] Wanted someone to take care of me
- [ ] Pregnancy
- [ ] Slid into the relationship while cohabitating
- [ ] Financial reasons
- [ ] To obtain US citizenship or help the other person obtain it
- [ ] Thought it would make my life better
- [ ] Other (explain):

What is your understanding of why one or more of these reasons for marrying may have caused your relationship to struggle and eventually end?

Which of your adaptive behaviors could have contributed to the end of your marriage?

What do you know about that now?

Which adaptive behaviors contributed to you choosing your partner?

The Match

Were you really meant for one another to begin with? It is important to be mature enough at the time of coupling up to be able to carefully assess a potential partner regardless of how much you may believe you are in love and want to marry that person. Sometimes there are issues you may have known about (or should have known) before marrying in the first place but either ignored or minimized. Many times, during the dating process the other person offers up disturbing information but it is glossed over... the proverbial red flag.

Do you believe that you were each mature enough at the time of committing to each other to understand what such a commitment would entail? Explain.

Were there things about this person that you now can admit were red flags- things you had seen prior to committing to each other? If yes, explain.

Knowing now what your relationship was like, what are your takeaways for your future self?

Rumination

Some people get stuck in a mental trap. They start thinking about their Ex or something about the relationship and they think about it over and over and over again.

The official definition:

Rumination involves repetitive thinking or dwelling on negative feelings and distress and their causes and consequences. The repetitive, negative aspect of rumination can contribute to the development of depression or anxiety and can worsen existing conditions.

Get clear on your rumination

What do you ruminate about?

What questions or things do you wonder, over and over?

What triggers the rumination?

Mark the days and times when you tend to ruminate the most.

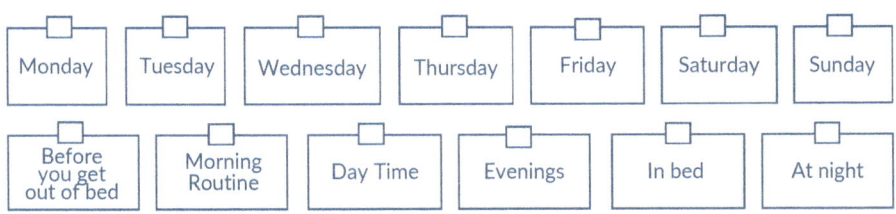

| Monday | Tuesday | Wednesday | Thursday | Friday | Saturday | Sunday |

| Before you get out of bed | Morning Routine | Day Time | Evenings | In bed | At night |

What do you do to get yourself out of the rumination?

Is there a consistency to your ruminations?

Some people create a movie of how they hope their future might go. What is that movie that you are creating?

What are some negative traits about your Ex?

Regret vs Guilt

Make a mistake? Release the guilt, remember the lesson.

Regret: "I wish I knew then what I know now"
Guilt: "I knew it was wrong when I was doing it"

People often confuse regret and guilt. It's an important distinction. They say I feel guilty about what happened or something they did. But more often than not, they regret things they said or did that resulted in the ending of a relationship. They simply didn't know or understand what the result would be. Affairs are something that most people feel guilty about. They knew it was wrong and they did it anyway. It went against their values, morals or code of ethics.

Reflect on your ruminations. Do you regret certain things in the relationship or do you feel guilty?

False Guilt is a feeling of guilt for something that is not in your control or doesn't violate your values. It can also be a fear of disapproval in disguise. For example, you might feel false guilt if you're late for an appointment because of an accident, or if you feel guilty for having a had a negative impact on someone. Reflect on your previous thoughts. Are they false guilt?

Can you see how you might turn your thoughts and ruminations into regrets and how that is a healthier way to move forward? Explain it below.

Anxiety and Depression

> "Anxiety is about the future, depression is about the past"

For people struggling with anxiety their mind goes down a path that confuses the difference between something that MIGHT happen and something that WILL happen.

The Habit Loop

When we get anxious often there is a mental habit loop that a person gets into. The first step is simply to become AWARE of this loop:

What Habit do you want to break?

Stage	Make it, to Break It	Make it, To Build It
Cue	Invisible	Obvious
Craving	Unattractive	Attractive
Response	Hard	Easy
Reward	Unsatisfying	Satisfying

The Feelings Compass

> "If you don't know what you are feeling you don't have a compass."

The Basic Feelings Compass

When we are feeling "good" our needs are being met. When people are asked how they are feeling they usually respond with "good" (even though "good" isn't a feeling"). However, when we aren't "good" people will say "ok", or "hanging in there", or something similar. In other words, something is wrong. When something is wrong it means our needs aren't being met.

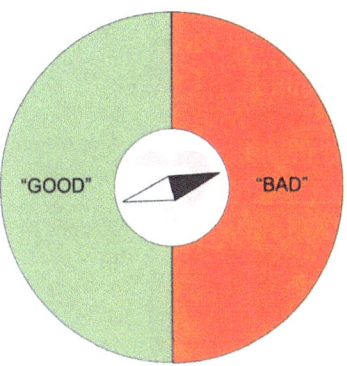

Now feelings aren't "good" or "bad" but we are referring to how people tend to interpret their feelings. They don't like feeling "bad" and they like feeling "good".

Feelings are Signposts

When working with people that are going through divorce one of the first things that stands out is how hard it is for people to identify WHAT they are feeling.

We find that most people are only aware of a few basic feelings: sad glad, mad, and afraid. They may use synonyms but this is often the range of their feelings vocabulary.

We want to help you expand your feelings vocabulary because when you learn to pay attention to what is happening in your body (your emotions) you can use these to understand what to do about it. You learn how to RESPOND to the world around you instead of REACT to your environment. By learning your feelings you gain control. You also are better able to communicate to others your experience which improves relationships.

Emotions vs feelings

The terms "feelings" and "emotions" are often used interchangeably, but they refer to different aspects of our psychological experience. Here's a breakdown of the differences:

	Emotions	Feelings
Definition	Emotions are complex psychological states that involve three distinct components: a subjective experience, a physiological response, and a behavioral or expressive response.	Feelings are the conscious experience of emotional reactions. They are the subjective interpretation of emotions.
Origin	Emotions are usually automatic responses to external stimuli and are often linked to evolutionary survival mechanisms.	Feelings arise from the brain's interpretation of emotions and can be influenced by personal experiences, beliefs, and memories.
Duration	Emotions are typically intense and short-lived.	Feelings tend to last longer than emotions and can persist as long as they are being thought about or dwelled upon.
Examples	Fear, anger, happiness, and sadness.	Feeling anxious, feeling content, feeling lonely, and feeling hopeful.

In other words, emotions are automatic responses to stimuli, while feelings are our personal interpretation of these emotional responses. Understanding the distinction can help individuals better manage your emotional well-being and responses to various life situations.

The Feelings Compass

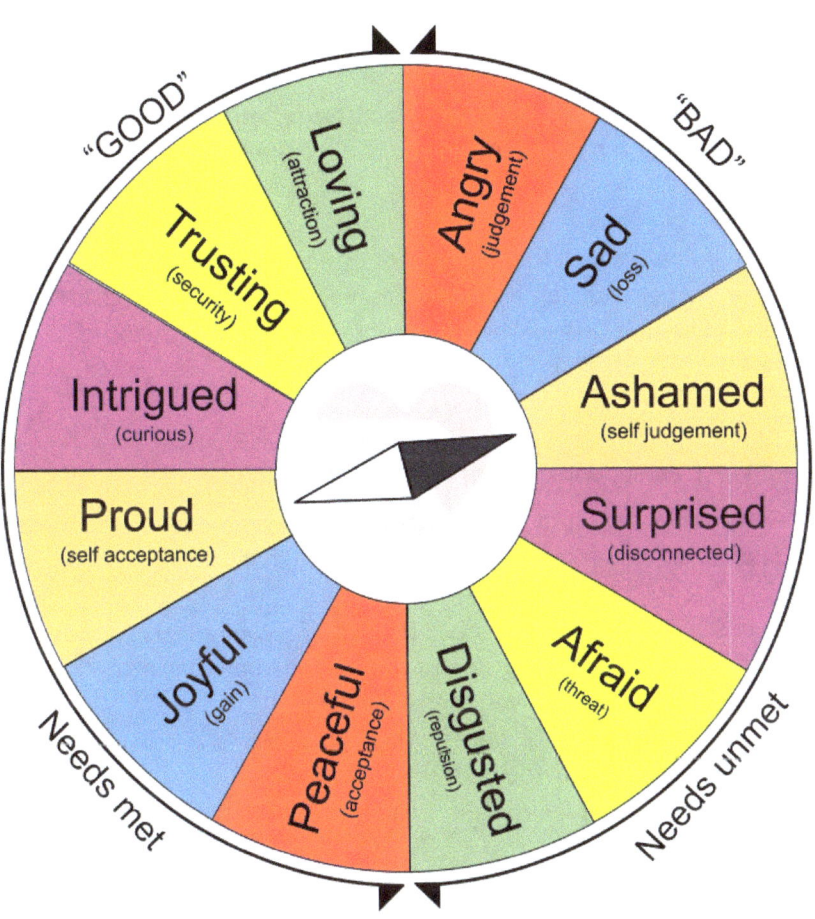

The Intermediate Feelings Compass

How to read the Feelings Compass

The first step is to learn the 6 "bad" feelings on the right side: anger, sadness, shame, surprise/shock, fear, and disgust. In the following pages we are going to go into greater detail on each of these so that first you can recognize them and second, so that you can then know what to do for each. Each feeling has different ways of dealing with them.

In the "Level 2" Feelings Compass you will see in small letters of each feeling and how to explain what the feeling "is".

Now if you look on the left side there are also 6 "good" feelings: Love, trust, intrigue, pride, joy, and peace. Again you will see the small letters near each feeling.

If you draw a line through the center of the compass you will see that the two feelings on the right and left are opposites. For example, the opposite of anger, which is judgment, is peace, which is acceptance. The opposite of fear, which is a threat, is trust, which is security.

The MISTAKE most people make:

People often think that if they are angry then they just need to stop being angry in order to be peaceful. It doesn't work like that.

In order to be free of anger, you need to EXPRESS your anger. You need to move it out of you. You can't just ignore them and hope they go away. Once you express your anger then you can explore the next step - what needs are or were not being met. THEN you can move from the right side to the left side of the compass towards peace.

You will learn about feelings in the upcoming pages and in the classes.

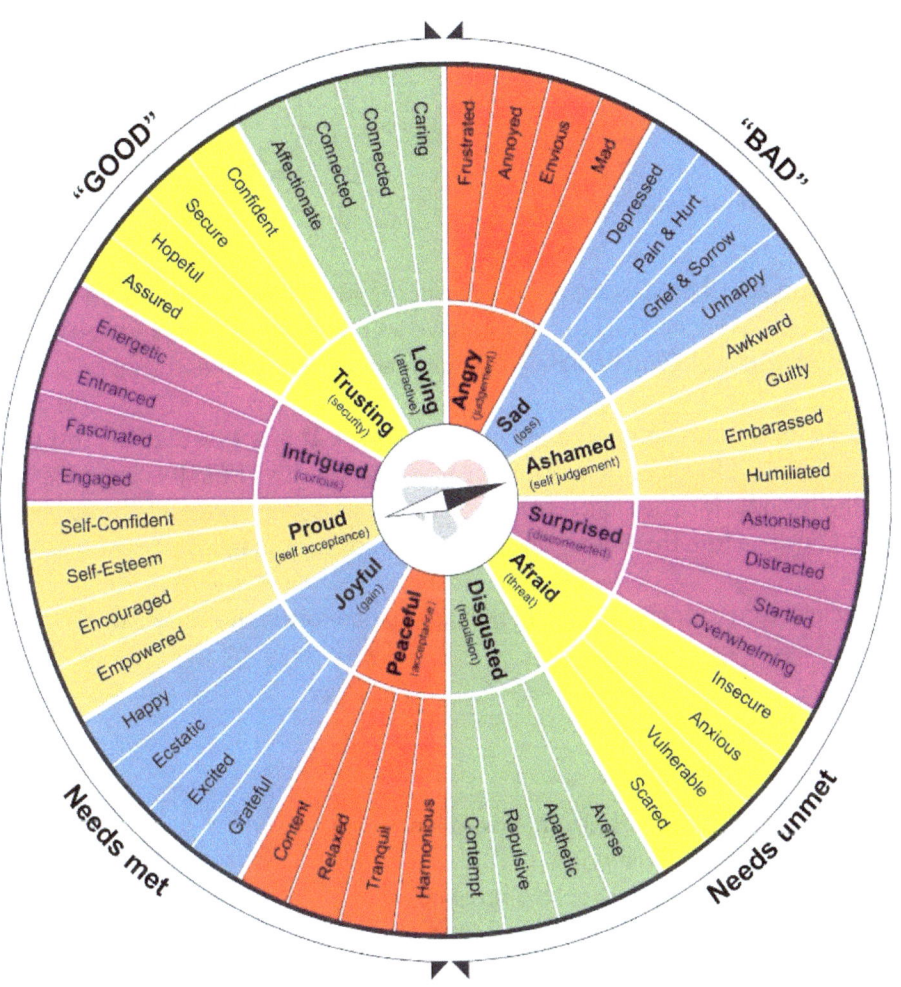

The Advanced Feelings Compass

The Emotional Broken Leg

From Kevin: When I was going through my divorce I leaned on my friends and family A LOT. In fact, it was too much for them. I was in such pain and I wanted them to take it away. However I was one of the first of my friends to divorce and no one really knew how to help me. The most common suggestion from my support system was "You just have to move on". I describe this as having an "Emotional Broken Leg".

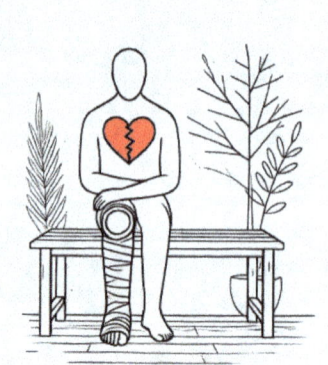

If I had an actual broken leg no one would suggest "just move on". They would say, "GO TO THE HOSPITAL". If you have an Emotional Broken Leg don't try to "Move On" until you heal the "difficult feelings" like grief and anger.

Emotional wounds are hard to detect and to heal. This is why the Self Test we offer is so helpful. If you haven't done it yet. DO IT. It's FREE. It is like an x-ray at the hospital for your leg. It helps you see what is going on inside of you emotionally. From there you can figure out what to do next.

Now let's turn to these "difficult feelings" that are often the source of the emotional broken leg.

Sadness

Most people dealing with divorce experience intense sadness at some point.
Heartbreak from any relationship breakup is a loss, and as we know from the Feelings Compass, sadness is loss.

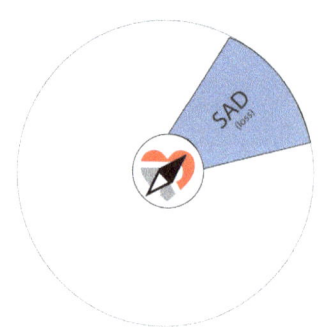

So what is **GRIEF?**
It is an intense version of sadness. It is still a loss but it is more acute and more painful.

	Sadness	Grief
Nature	A basic human emotion that is a natural response to situations that are upsetting, disappointing, or stressful.	A deeper, more intense emotional response specifically related to significant losses
Duration	It is usually temporary and tends to diminish with time or positive changes in circumstances	Can be prolonged and is often more complex. The intensity can fluctuate over time.
Triggers	Can be caused by a variety of situations such as a bad day at work, a minor argument with a friend, or a disappointing event.	Usually triggered by a profound loss and can be re-triggered by reminders of the loss
Intensity	Generally less intense than grief and can be alleviated by engaging in enjoyable activities or through social support.	More intense and pervasive, often affecting multiple aspects of life, including physical health, relationships, and day-to-day functioning.
Function	Helps individuals process and respond to difficult situations, encouraging reflection and sometimes prompting change.	Serves as a crucial process for coming to terms with a significant loss and finding a way to move forward. It often requires more support and time to work through.

Divorce is a loss of expectations. When you married you had hopes and dreams for a different future. The grief from heartbreak is about letting go of those LIFE goals and dreams. It is about letting go of a person you loved so deeply.

Grief is cumulative. There are lots of losses in life and if we don't let them go then they add up.

Angela had just had her second child when her mother died. Her husband was a partner in a successful law firm. She had to continue to take care of her kids. She didn't have time to grieve. 10 years later when she and husband divorced she was overwhelmed with sadness. Her life had fallen apart and she couldn't seem to move forward. Why? Because she hadn't grieved, both the passing of her mother & the ending of her marriage.

Grief needs to be addressed. It doesn't just fade with time. What happens is that people get used to the sadness but it sits there under the surface until you deal with it.

So deal with it now, or later, but one way or the other, the only way out is through.

Your grief score _____

If you took the self test write in your score here.

If you scored less than 80 percentile on the self test then you have grief that needs to be dealt with in order to move forward. The lower the score the more important it is that you put your attention on it.

HOW LONG DOES IT TAKE TO GET OVER A DIVORCE?

> **"If you take the time it takes, it takes less time"** - Julie M

There is a myth that it takes 1 year of grieving for every 5 years you were married. This is utter nonsense. There is no formula for grieving. However, we know that people that avoid it and hope it goes away find that it takes them longer than dealing with it head on. (See: The Obstacle is the Way)

Types of grief

There are several types of grief
- Anticipatory grief – when a person is expecting or anticipating a loss
- Acute grief – sudden, immediate reaction to a loss (often experienced by the Resister)
- Chronic grief – long-term effects of a loss
- Complicated grief – when normal grieving processes become distorted or difficult to manage
- Distorted grief – when someone attempts to deny the reality of a loss. (Also common for the Resister)

It is normal to experience very intense grief during a divorce. You may experience one or more of the above types. However, diagnosing which "kind" you have takes away from simply experiencing the grief.

If you are sad, be sad. Don't try to change it, fix it, or minimize it.

Divorce creates grief in a number of ways. We don't just lose the person we planned to spend the rest of our life with. We have loss in a number of ways that are often unexpected.

Losses due to divorce:
(check the boxes for ones that apply to you)

☐ **Loss of Your Partner:** This is the primary, tangible loss of someone important, often recognized as the absence of their physical presence. Living with someone for years and then being without them can make us miss their physical existence. Changes in mental functioning, physical capabilities, or personality can also make it feel like the person is no longer the one you once knew and loved.

☐ **Loss of Identity:** Being with someone for many years creates a WE identity rather than ME. In a breakup, the loss of WE means accepting a new identity as ME, which can be confusing and leave us feeling alone and unmoored from something we relied on for so long.

☐ **Loss of Purpose:** As a partner, your self-worth may have been tied to caring for your loved one. When a marriage ends, you lose both a spouse and the role of caretaker, leaving two voids. This can initially make you feel like nothing matters anymore, leading to a challenging task of redefining your sense of purpose.

☐ **Loss of Family and Friends:** During a breakup, friends and family may feel confused and unsure of how to support you. Often, they care about both parties and may "pick a side," leading to feelings of isolation. You might experience loneliness from withdrawing from previous routines and relationships and from moving away from your support network. Family and friends may retreat, not knowing how to respond to your changed life.

☐ **Loss of Physical Health:** The overwhelming process of divorce can lead to under-eating or overeating, changes in exercise habits, and sleep disturbances. The physical and emotional strain of managing life while caring for yourself and possibly children can put divorcees at serious risk for health problems.

Black Water Pond (Excerpt), by Mary Oliver

To live in this world

you must be able
to do three things:
to love what is mortal;
to hold it

against your bones knowing
your own life depends on it;
and, when the time comes to let it go,
to let it go.

The Well of Grief, by David Whyte

Those who will not slip beneath
the still surface on the well of grief,

turning down through its black water
to the place we cannot breathe,

will never know the source from which we drink,
the secret water, cold and clear,

nor find in the darkness glimmering,
the small round coins,
thrown by those who wished for something else

What do these poems evoke in you?

The Goodbye Letter

The following exercise is one of the most powerful tools for letting go. A Goodbye Letter is a letter that is written with kindness and understanding towards your ex. You are not blaming or accusing. This is you separating. It is a chance to move the thoughts in your head to something tangible outside of you. It is important to spend time on this. You are going to write about the things that you are going to miss, the things you are letting go of, and more. You are saying goodbye to the hopes and dreams you had for your future with this person. It is not angry. Save that for later.

Also, for many this is a VERY challenging assignment. We get it. It IS hard.

Some suggestions for starting each statement:
- Goodbye to....
- What I had and will never have again...
- What I miss...
- What I counted on was....
- I feel most sad about....
- I have a lot of grief because....
- I planned on.......

Whatever you do with your letter, make it your own. This is for you. Consider it to be like a funeral for your relationship. You might envision yourself speaking to a group of people at a funeral and telling them in kind words what you are letting go of and what you will miss. Do NOT send or read it to your ex. Here's why, if you write it for them you will filter or be thinking of how they will receive it. THIS IS FOR YOU. Do this exercise for your own healing.

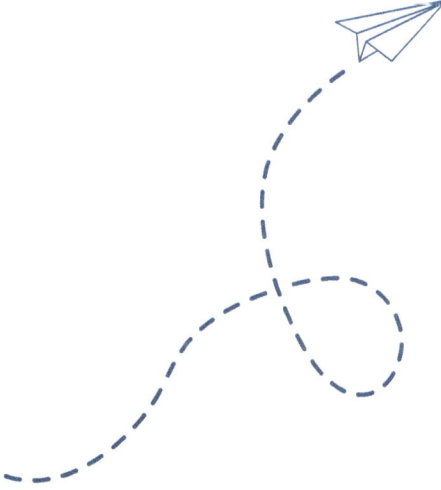

My Goodbye Letter

My Goodbye Letter

My Goodbye Letter

Marriage Autopsy - Compatibility

Were you and your partner friends? Best friends? Yes or no?
How did this affect you positively or negatively?

Did you have enough in common to make life fun? i.e. Interests, activities or hobbies?
What did you share in these areas?

Did you share friendships?
Did you go out together socially as a couple?
Did you or your partner only socialize with personal friends and not with each other?
Did your friends contribute positively or negatively to your marriage?
Did they support your marriage? Explain any of these.

Which of the following did you have similar and compatible attitudes about?

☐ Life
☐ Religion
☐ Politics
☐ Having children or how
   to raise them
☐ Drugs & alcohol use
☐ Finances
☐ Extended family
☐ Goals
☐ Work
☐ Kind of home to live in
☐ Sex

☐ Travel
☐ Care for your home
☐ Vacations
☐ The environment
☐ Lifestyle
☐ Recreation
☐ The definition of
☐ Commitment
☐ Physical and/or mental
☐ Illness
☐ Amount of time you need
   to spend together or apart

What can your answer tell you about the strength or weakness of your relationship?

Did you both respect each other's differences? If not, how did that affect your relationship?

Anger

Anger is the MOST misunderstood emotion. People think they know what it is but as we explore it with people often they realize that they don't truly recognize it or value it.

In our group programs we focus on helping people to use their anger in a positive way rather than avoid it or use it in a destructive way.

Also, many people think they shouldn't be angry but they are. So what do they do? They suppress it, they hide it, they try to explain it away with logic.

Others use anger as a sword. They are quick to use it and to let other people know it. They think that they have a right to share their anger, regardless of the effects.

Your Anger Score _____

So what is anger?

Anger is a natural, intense emotional response to perceived threats, frustrations, or injustices. It is a complex emotion that can range from mild irritation to intense fury and rage. Anger can be triggered by both internal and external factors, such as personal experiences, interactions with others, or even thoughts and memories.

Some would say that anger is when a line has been crossed. In other words, it is the emotion we feel when a behavior, thought, or verbal message goes from "okay" to "NOT okay". There is judgment in anger.

Here's a secret: <u>anger is a secondary emotion and it points to unmet needs.</u>

When you feel angry, what
do you do?

Anger Spectrum

Where do you feel it in
your body?

How long does it take you to
rebound when you are
extremely angry?

What strategies do you use
when you are angry and
don't want to be?

Key Aspects of Anger:

Physiological Response: When angry, the body undergoes various physiological changes, such as increased heart rate, elevated blood pressure, and the release of adrenaline. These responses are part of the body's "fight or flight" reaction.

Psychological Impact: Anger can affect mental well-being, leading to feelings of frustration, hostility, and resentment. If not managed properly, it can contribute to mental health issues like anxiety and depression.

Behavioral Expression: Anger can be expressed in various ways, including verbal outbursts, physical aggression, or passive-aggressive behavior. How an individual expresses anger often depends on their personality, upbringing, and social context.

Triggers: Common triggers for anger include feeling threatened, frustrated, powerless, or wronged. Situations like conflicts with others, unmet needs, and perceived injustices can also provoke anger.

Consequences: While anger can be a motivating force for addressing issues and advocating for oneself, unmanaged anger can have negative consequences. It can damage relationships, lead to poor decision-making, and result in physical health problems.

Using the 5 characteristics above, journal about your anger and how it shows up for you.

The 5 Ways to Express Anger

Usually people have a "go to" method of expressing anger. In this section we are going to explore the different ways people express anger and show you how to release anger such that it improves relationships rather than erodes them.

Suppressed anger refers to the internalization of anger, where individuals consciously or unconsciously deny or push down their feelings of anger. This can lead to internal stress, anxiety, and even physical health issues because the anger is not addressed or expressed. It shows up as a repression of feelings, denial of anger, possible physical symptoms like headaches or stomach aches, and emotional outbursts at seemingly unrelated events due to the buildup of tension.

Open anger is the clear and direct expression of anger, where individuals openly show their feelings through verbal or physical actions. This type of anger is usually noticeable by others and can involve shouting, arguing, or even physical aggression. It shows up through loud and direct expressions, visible frustration, physical gestures like clenching fists, and potential for confrontation or conflict with others.

Passive anger is expressed indirectly, often through behaviors that are meant to avoid direct confrontation. People exhibiting passive anger might use sarcasm, procrastination, or other passive-aggressive behaviors to express their displeasure without directly acknowledging their anger. It shows up through indirect communication, sarcasm, subtle insults, procrastination, and a general unwillingness to engage in direct conflict.

Assertive anger is the constructive expression of anger where individuals communicate their feelings openly and honestly without being aggressive. This type of anger is characterized by a balance between expressing anger and respecting others, aiming to resolve the underlying issue. It shows up as clear and respectful communication, focus on problem-solving, maintaining control, and an emphasis on mutual respect and understanding.

Dropped anger involves the conscious and healthy release of anger in ways that do not harm oneself or others. This can include activities like physical exercise, creative outlets, or talking through feelings with a trusted person. It can also be called "Dropping It" which is different from suppressed anger in that it is simply gone versus "stored for later".

The first 3 types of anger are ways that we express anger DISRESPECTFULLY. They don't value the other person that we are angry at. They don't give us a way to interact and communicate to improve our relationship, instead they create more distance.

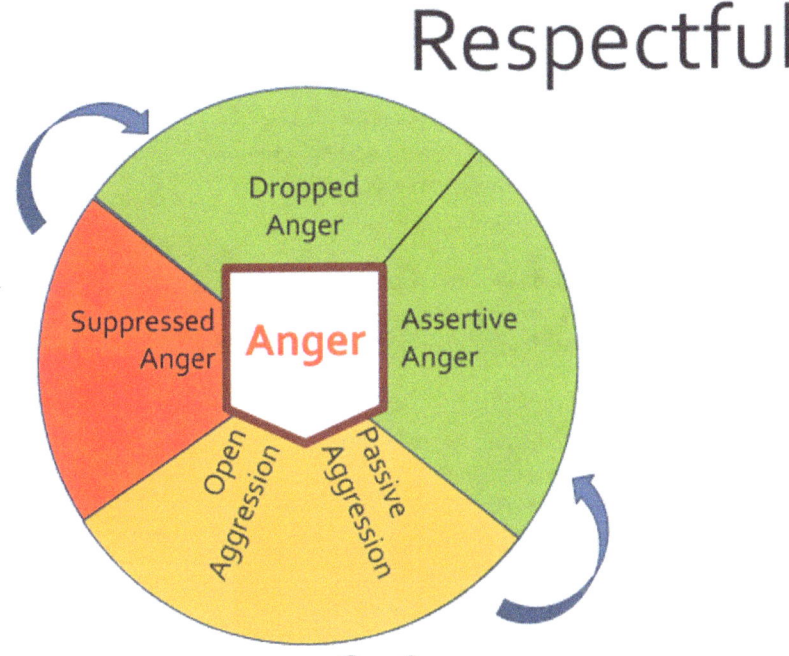

The second 2 types of anger ARE respectful. They don't cause harm. In fact they acknowledge the feeling and then allow the person with the anger to DO something with it.

By understanding this we can look at the disrespectful types of anger and with training, learn to transform it into a respectful expression of anger. Most often Open Aggression and Passive Aggression can be turned into Assertive Anger. Suppressed Anger can be turned into Dropped Anger or Assertive Anger.

The Anger Letter

Now you are going to write an anger letter. Write about any event, situation, comment, attitude, belief, behavior, habit that your ex made or had that had a negative effect on you.

Some suggestions for starting each statement:
- "when you said ... it really hurt and I became really angry
- The way you were always so ... affected me so I often felt ..._and then I got angry
- I hid my anger from you because...
- I was aggravated when you...
- My frustration level was very high because...
- I was perturbed, when you did.....said....and I became really angry
- When I felt angry, what I usually did was...
- I held back my anger when ...
- I got really angry when...
- My Father/Mother/Ex dealt with anger by...
- Growing up my way of dealing with anger was...
- When I am angry, I feel it in .... (identify where in your body you tend to feel when you are angry)
- Anger scares me when...
- If I really express myself when angry I might...
- My anger turns in to aggression when...
- When I am reactive I express my anger by...
- I need my anger to...
- Usually my message when angry is ...
- In the past being vulnerable when angry was ...
- I turn my anger on myself when...
- My breathing is affected when I am angry how...
- What REALLY makes me angry is...
- I realize how much of our relationship I spent feeling _____ and angry.
- I numbed so many of my feelings because _____

Try these other feelings instead of just using the word angry:
Exasperated – Impatient - Upset - Agitated – Indignant - Infuriated - Resentful - Outraged - Furious – Irate...

The goal is to express as much of the angry feelings/sentiments as possible in your letter. Swear words are perfectly normal and acceptable if you want to use them. Don't hold back. This is for you.

Whatever you do with your letter, make it your own. This if for you. Do NOT send or read it to your ex. You will have the opportunity for you to read it in class, if you choose.

My Anger Letter

My Anger Letter

My Anger Letter

Marriage Autopsy - Respect

Did you allow each other time alone when it was needed?

Were each of you able to entertain yourselves when the other was unable to be present?

What did each of you do when you needed to be alone for a while?

Did you trust each other? Y / N If no, explain.

Marriage Autopsy - Respect

Were you able to have empathy, respect, understanding, patience, compassion, and sensitivity for your partner and they for you? Y/N If no, explain.

Were you able to confide in each other on a regular basis? YES/NO If no, explain

Were you able to share ALL your feelings: sad, happiness, anger, fear, shame etc.?

If not, which feelings were hard to share and why do you think this was difficult?

Shame

Brene Brown has researched shame for years. Her understanding of it has changed the world. One of our favorite phrases for her is the idea that "Shame is like quicksand, the more you try to get out alone the deeper you sink. You need others to help you get out."

Shame is the fear of disconnection.
It is the belief that there is something wrong with me.

Brene Brown: "I define shame as the intensely painful feeling or experience of believing that we are flawed and therefore unworthy of love and belonging— something we've experienced, done, or failed to do makes us unworthy of connection."

Many people are deeply ashamed that they are getting divorced. The thought is that there must be something wrong with me if I'm divorced. I'm not worthy of love or I have failed in some way.

Guilt

Often the person that Initiates the divorce feels guilty.

> "Guilt is holding something we've done or failed to do up against our values and feeling psychological discomfort." -Brené Brown

Often the person that makes the decision to end the marriage struggles because it goes against their values or beliefs. However, they often feel like divorce is the only option to honor themselves and not continue in a relationship in which they are deeply unhappy.

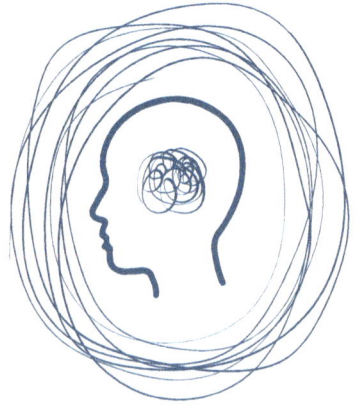

Surprise/Shock

Surprise and shock are common reactions when a marriage ends, often hitting individuals unexpectedly, even if there were signs of trouble. The initial phase of shock is a natural response to the sudden disruption of what one thought was a stable part of their life. It's not just the end of a relationship but the abrupt halt to shared dreams, routines, and a sense of security. Physically, one might feel numbness or an inability to breathe deeply, while emotionally, this can translate to disbelief, confusion, and detachment from reality. These feelings, though overwhelming, are normal and part of adjusting to a new reality.

The occurrence of surprise and shock is rooted in the abrupt change to one's expectations and life plans. Even if there were conflicts or problems in the marriage, the finality of divorce often catches people off guard. The mind grapples with the disconnect between anticipated and unfolding realities, leading to a period of denial where acceptance is difficult. Navigating through this phase is crucial for moving forward. Understanding these reactions as a natural part of the grieving process allows individuals to be kinder to themselves, laying the groundwork for future healing. Engaging in the Rebuilders Support and Recovery Groups can help with processing these emotions without judgment and can facilitate a healthier transition through this challenging time.

Disgust

Disgust is a powerful and often surprising emotion that can surface during a divorce. It typically arises from feelings of betrayal, disappointment, or a profound disconnection from one's former partner. This emotion can manifest when reflecting on hurtful actions, broken promises, or behaviors that now seem intolerable. Disgust may also stem from recognizing aspects of the relationship or the partner that were previously overlooked or tolerated. This intense emotional reaction serves as a protective mechanism, distancing oneself from what is perceived as harmful or unacceptable.

The experience of disgust during divorce is deeply personal and can significantly impact one's emotional landscape. It may lead to a sense of revulsion towards the ex-partner, making interactions challenging and potentially fueling conflict.

Acknowledging and understanding this emotion is crucial for personal healing. It's important to process these feelings constructively, possibly through therapy or support groups, to avoid being consumed by negativity. By addressing disgust, individuals can work towards releasing these intense emotions and moving towards a place of acceptance and emotional freedom.

Numbing

Looking back at our Feelings Compass we find that people often want to avoid the "difficult feelings" and instead focus on feeling the good feelings. Unfortunately, if we deny grief and anger, we are suppressing, depressing, or repressing them. We are numbing those feelings to avoid the emotional pain. This is not a good long term strategy.

> **"You cannot numb one feeling without numbing them all". - Nick Meima**

Many people numb themselves to avoid the pain. It is a very useful short term strategy. Here are some common ways:

- ☐ Work excessively
- ☐ Clean excessively
- ☐ Stay up late
- ☐ Play video games
- ☐ Date excessively

- ☐ Sleep excessively
- ☐ Eat or diet excessively
- ☐ Exercise excessively
- ☐ Addictions
- ☐ Others...

How have you been numbing yourself?

Now let's turn our attention to the left side of the Feelings Compass, the side that people WANT to feel.

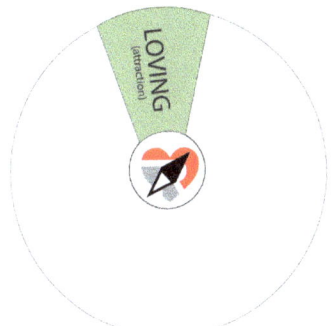

Love is a Verb -*Ally D.*

Love is a confusing emotion for most people. It means different things to different people. "I LOVE YOU" carries a lot of weight for some people. For others they say it without distinction or heaviness. It is a way to convey "I care about you".

What does "I LOVE YOU" mean to you?

Attachment vs Love

Love	Attachment
Unconditional: Genuine love is unconditional and selfless. It is caring deeply for someone and wanting the best for them, regardless of personal gain.	Conditional: Attachment often comes with conditions and expectations. It may rely on the other person fulfilling specific needs or desires.
Freedom: Love respects individuality and freedom. It allows space for both partners to grow independently and encourages personal development.	Dependency: Attachment can lead to dependency, where one's happiness and well-being become overly reliant on the other person.
Trust and Respect: True love is built on mutual trust and respect. It values open communication and understanding.	Possessiveness: Attachment can involve possessiveness and control, leading to jealousy and fear of losing the person.
Supportive: Love is supportive, fostering a nurturing environment where both partners feel safe and valued.	Insecurity: Attachment is often rooted in insecurity and the fear of being alone or abandoned
Joy and Contentment: Love brings a sense of joy and contentment, creating positive emotions and experiences.	Short-Term: Attachment can be fleeting and may not withstand challenges. It often fades when the initial excitement or need is no longer met.
Long-Lasting: Love is enduring and can withstand challenges and changes over time.	Emotional Rollercoaster: Attachment can create an emotional rollercoaster, with highs and lows based on the relationship's status and the other person's actions.

Do you think your partner was in love with you or was he/she attached to you?

Were you in love with your partner or were you attached?

The Types of Love

Love can be categorized into different types including romantic and platonic love.
Romantic love often involves physical intimacy with a partner or spouse, while platonic love can be affectionate or passionate but doesn't include sexual feelings. Here are some other types of love. **Write the names of people that you have this kind of love with in the margins.**

Eros: A passionate, sexual, and physical love named after the Greek god of love

Agape: A selfless and altruistic form of everlasting love that can apply to everyone and everything, even without the expectation of reciprocation

Ludus: A childlike and flirtatious love that's common in the beginning stages of a relationship, characterized by teasing, laughter, and playful motives

Philia: An affectionate love between equals, often strong friendship or brotherly love, that's built on honesty and understanding

Storge: An affectionate, naturally occurring, and unforced love that family members have for one another, such as parents and children

Pragma: A type of romantic love that focuses on compatibility and steadiness, and has moved beyond the powerful urges of the beginning stages of a relationship

Obsessive love (not real love): A preoccupation with capturing and controlling another person who is physically, spiritually, or emotionally unavailable

The Spectrum of Love

Here are some words that are often associated with love and different ways that we describe them. It is helpful for people to expand their vocabulary around love and understand that we can describe love in many different ways. Underline the words that you commonly use. Circle words that you would like to use more often.

Affection

Adoration

Passion

Devotion

Caring

Tenderness

Intimacy

Compassion

Fondness

Amour

Romance

Heartfelt

Commitment

Empathy

Attachment

Warmth

Endearment

Loyalty

Trust

Connection

Unity

Bliss

Happiness

Joy

Kindness

Desire

Cherish

Attraction

Devoted

Gratitude

Togetherness

Belonging

Respect

Harmony

Sweetheart

Admiration

Embrace

Sentiment

Nurture

Support

Engagement

Infatuation

Intimacy

Kind Hearted

Loving

Yearning

Compassionate

Soulmate

Generosity

Serenity

Love Spectrum

Reflect on love.

What does "I love you" mean to you?

What does it imply?

If someone says it to you but you don't love them, what would you say?

Trust

A lot of people say "I trust you" or "I don't trust you". But in what way? The 7 Types of Trust developed by Brene Brown help us to see trust more clearly by distinguishing that there are different types of trust.

> **"You take the stairs up and the elevator down." - Kevin V**

B _____

R _____

A _____

V _____

I _____

N _____

G _____

Who don't you trust and why?

Do you trust yourself?

The 7 Types of Trust

Boundaries	I trust if: • you are clear about your boundaries and you hold them and • you are clear about my boundaries and you respect them.
Reliability	• I can only trust you if you do what you say you are going to do. Over and over and over again. • We have to be clear on our expectations and capabilities so that we don't take on too much.
Accountability	• I can only trust you if when you make a mistake you own it, apologize for it and make amends. • I can only trust you if when I make a mistake that I am allowed to own it, apologize for it and make amends.
Vault	• What I share with you, confidentially, you will hold in confidence. • What you share with me, I will hold in confidence.
Integrity	• Choosing courage over comfort. • Choosing what's right over what's easy. • Practicing your values, not just professing your values.
Non-Judgment	• I can fall apart, be in struggle, ask for help and not be judged by you. • You can fall apart, be in struggle, ask for help and not be judged by me.
Generosity	Our relationship is only trusting if you can only assume the most generous thing about me, and I about you.

Intrigue

Intrigue, often associated with mystery and curiosity, plays a significant role in the journey through and after divorce. When individuals face the end of a marriage, they are thrust into a new chapter of life filled with unknowns. This uncertainty can be daunting, but it also presents an opportunity for growth and exploration. Cultivating intrigue allows individuals to view their post-divorce life as an adventure rather than a setback. By embracing curiosity, they can explore new interests, form new relationships, and discover aspects of themselves that were previously overshadowed by their marital identity. This mindset shift helps transform the experience of divorce from a period of loss to one of potential and self-discovery.

Moreover, intrigue can be a powerful tool for healing and resilience. When individuals maintain a sense of curiosity, they are more likely to engage in activities that bring joy and fulfillment, helping to mitigate feelings of loneliness and despair that often accompany divorce. Intrigue encourages them to ask questions, seek new experiences, and remain open to possibilities, fostering a sense of hope and excitement for the future. This proactive approach to life can significantly enhance emotional well-being, making the recovery process smoother and more empowering. By cultivating intrigue, individuals can rebuild their lives with a renewed sense of purpose and enthusiasm, ultimately leading to a more vibrant and satisfying post-divorce existence.

Wherever you are right now, look around the room and gaze at an object. Get curious about it.

- How was it made?
- Where was it made?
- How many people touched it before you?
- What do you like about it?

Pride

Healthy pride is a positive sense of self-respect and self-worth that arises from acknowledging and appreciating one's achievements, abilities, and intrinsic value. Unlike arrogance or hubris, which involves an inflated sense of self-importance, healthy pride is rooted in a balanced and realistic appraisal of oneself. It involves recognizing personal accomplishments, setting and achieving goals, and maintaining a sense of dignity and self-respect even in the face of challenges. Healthy pride fosters confidence and resilience, enabling individuals to navigate life's ups and downs with a stable sense of self-assurance and integrity.

Cultivating healthy pride involves several key practices. First, it's important to regularly reflect on and celebrate personal achievements, no matter how small. This can be done through journaling, sharing successes with supportive friends or family, or simply taking a moment to acknowledge one's efforts and progress. Second, setting realistic and meaningful goals helps build a sense of accomplishment and forward momentum. Third, practicing self-compassion is crucial; this means treating oneself with kindness and understanding, especially during setbacks or failures. Finally, surrounding oneself with positive and supportive people who encourage and affirm one's worth can reinforce healthy pride. By engaging in these practices, individuals can develop a robust and positive sense of pride that supports their overall well-being and personal growth.

What recent accomplishments or efforts am I proud of, and how have they contributed to my growth and well-being?

How do I respond to setbacks or failures, and what steps can I take to maintain my sense of self-worth during challenging times?

Who are the people in my life that support and affirm my value, and how can I nurture these relationships to reinforce my healthy pride?

Joy

Joy is a profound sense of happiness and contentment that transcends fleeting pleasures or superficial gratifications. It is a deep, abiding feeling that arises from within, often linked to a sense of fulfillment and connection to oneself and others. Joy can be found in simple moments of life, such as spending time with loved ones, engaging in meaningful activities, or simply appreciating the beauty of nature. Unlike temporary bursts of happiness, joy is a stable and enduring state that enhances overall well-being and life satisfaction.

> "It's not joy that makes us grateful, it's gratitude that makes us joyful."

One of the most effective ways to cultivate joy is through the practice of gratitude. When individuals regularly acknowledge and appreciate the positive aspects of their lives, they shift their focus from what is lacking to what is abundant. This shift in perspective fosters a greater sense of contentment and fulfillment. Practicing gratitude can be as simple as keeping a daily gratitude journal, where one lists things they are thankful for, or expressing appreciation to others. Over time, these practices build a mindset of gratitude, which naturally leads to increased joy. By recognizing and valuing the good in their lives, individuals can experience a deeper sense of joy and well-being, regardless of external circumstances.

Who are the people in my life that support and affirm my value, and how can I nurture these relationships to reinforce my healthy pride?

Reflect on a recent experience that brought you joy. What elements of that experience made it joyful, and how can you incorporate more of those elements into your daily life?

Who are the people in my life that I am grateful for, and how do their presence and actions contribute to my joy?
How can I express my gratitude to them?

Peace

Divorce often ushers in a period of significant chaos and upheaval, disrupting the familiar rhythms and routines of daily life. Amidst the emotional turmoil and logistical challenges, cultivating a sense of peace becomes essential. However, peace is not merely the absence of conflict or a state of calmness; it is about reaching a profound sense of acceptance with the world as it is. This means embracing the reality of one's circumstances, without resistance or denial. It involves recognizing that while the external world may be in flux, inner peace can still be achieved through a conscious decision to accept and navigate life's complexities with grace and resilience.

Cultivating peace is a deeply personal journey, focused on finding harmony within oneself rather than seeking to change others or external situations. It is not about forgiveness or condoning past actions but rather about coming to terms with the present moment and the self. Acceptance is key—acceptance of one's feelings, experiences, and the world around us. By practicing mindfulness, engaging in self-care, and fostering a compassionate inner dialogue, individuals can build a foundation of peace that sustains them through the turbulence of divorce. This inner peace allows for a more balanced and centered approach to life, enabling one to move forward with clarity and strength.

What aspects of my current situation can I accept as they are, and how can embracing this acceptance bring a sense of peace to my life?

In what ways can I nurture my mind and body to cultivate inner peace amidst the chaos of divorce? List specific activities or practices that help you feel centered and calm.

Reflect on a time when you felt a deep sense of peace despite external circumstances. What elements contributed to that feeling, and how can you recreate or sustain those elements in your present life?

The Needs Map

Underneath feelings are needs. Many people, when asked "What do you need?", have no idea how to respond. In this section we are going to link our Feelings Compass (page 66) with something called a Needs Map. Why? Because if you have a compass you need a map to understand your terrain. We are going to start with a very basic map of our needs. For example, we all have a need for love - to love and to be loved. We have a need to be autonomous but we also have a need to be connected with others. Many people are devastated from their divorce because they have the thought "I don't matter". They start to realize that all the years together don't mean as much to their partner as it does to them. When we examine our feelings we find that they point to what need is missing or being fulfilled. On the Feelings Compass we see that the right side feelings, the "difficult" feelings are because we have "unmet" needs. When we have feelings on the left side it is BECAUSE we have certain needs that ARE being met.

Life	Well-Being	Worth	Authenticity
Fullfilment	Trust	Capability	Autonomy
Love	Mutuality	Harmony	Wholeness

Which of the needs above are missing for you?

Which needs ARE being met?

The Advanced Needs Map

LIFE	WELL BEING	WORTH	AUTHENTICITY
Gratefulness	Health Sustenance	Value Recognition	Significance Expression
Awareness	Rejuvenation	Respect Success	Inspiration Purpose
Beauty Joy Mourning	Comfort Vitality	To Matter	Meaning Creativity
Presence	Energy Nourishment	Affirmation Gratitude	Originality
Appreciation	Rest Healing Relief	Appreciation	Congruence
Aesthetics	Protection	Acknowledgment	To Be Known
Celebration Humor			To Be Understood

FULFILLMENT	TRUST	CAPABILITY	AUTONOMY
Fun & Play	Stability Loyalty	Knowledge Competence	Independence
Aliveness	Commitment	Learning Awareness	Freedom Strength
Exploration	Predictability	To Understand	Privacy
Challenge	Reliability Safety	Confidence	Self-Determination
Spontaneity	Fidelity Order	Proficiency Growth	Control Choice
Pleasure Excitement	To Be Trusted	Wisdom Clarity	Liberty Leadership
Adventure			Courage Solitude
			Space

LOVE	MUTUALITY	HARMONY	WHOLENESS
Connection Intimacy	Care Cooperation	Peace Consideration	Integrity Fairness
Inclusion Empathy	Community	Balance Unity	Civility Responsibility
Communion	Contribution	Serenity Tranquility	Honesty
Closeness	Nurturance Help	Kindness Warmth	Truthfulness Justice
Acceptance	Support Service	Equanimity Ease	Equality Politeness
Belonging	Fellowship Giving	Accord Consensus	Courteousness
Understanding	Generosity		Accuracy
Compassion	Receiving		Accountability

The needs map on the previous page can be overwhelming. You may want many of them. However, write 10 needs that are particularly strong for you:

_____	_____
_____	_____
_____	_____
_____	_____
_____	_____

How can you get your needs met, without relying on someone else?

Needs List

Primary needs are defined as the needs beyond physical, that we need to meet in order to rebuild and heal. Note that the majority of needs on the Primary needs list, can only be met by you. If you meet them you will, you will experience fulfillment, satisfaction and be on the path to creating a wonderful life.

PRIMARY NEEDS

Self-Expression	To be Real/Authentic	Healthy Pleasure
Creativity	To be Self-Responsible	Intimacy
Touch	For Connection	Closeness
To be trusted	Mutuality	Self Love
To be trustworthy	Growth and Development	Self Compassion
To love	Fulfillment of potential	Self Acceptance

ADDITIONAL NEEDS

Interdependence

Belonging
Friendship
Love/caring
Attention
Comfort
Acceptance
To matter
To be "seen"
To be "heard"
Acknowledgement
Interdependence

Fulfillment

Contribution
Goals
Meaning
Unity
Compassion
Celebrate
Gratitude
Synergy
Discovery
Empowered
Equality/Mutuality
Learning
Beauty
Nature
Spirituality
Art/Music
Recreation

Personal Autonomy

Privacy
Career
Choice
Competence
Ability
Hobbies
Predictability
Order
Peace
Self-Determination
Independence

Identity

Identity is a core aspect of our existence, representing how we see ourselves and who we believe we are. In the context of divorce recovery, particularly within the RIFT Recovery process, the exploration of identity becomes a crucial phase once individuals have moved beyond the initial stages of processing thoughts and feelings. The first two stages involve navigating and healing from the intense emotions of grief, anger, and heartbreak, as well as reframing thoughts that are tethered to the past. As individuals progress and these intense emotions begin to subside, they turn a significant corner. At this juncture, they often find themselves confronting the profound question of "Who am I?"

In marriage, one's identity is often intertwined with their partner, creating a collective sense of "we." Divorce shatters this shared identity, leaving individuals to grapple with their singular self—transitioning from "we" to "me." Many people find that during their marriage, they lost a sense of their individual identity, having given so much of themselves to the relationship. Now, as they face life alone, they may feel uncertain about who they are as a single person. This new phase of identity involves rediscovering and re-establishing oneself. It is about learning to love and accept oneself, and truly feeling comfortable being alone in one's own skin. This phase is a journey of self-exploration and self-acceptance, laying the groundwork for a solid and healthy sense of self.

In the following pages of the workbook, we will delve into exercises designed to help you grow your sense of identity and reconnect with who they truly are. These exercises are structured to facilitate self-discovery, self-love, and self-acceptance. It is important to note, however, that attempting to jump directly into the identity phase without adequately addressing your past can be counterproductive. It is perfectly okay to work on one's identity while also addressing the past, but it is essential not to neglect the healing of past wounds. By understanding and honoring this process, you can build a stronger, more resilient sense of self, paving the way for a fulfilling and empowered future.

LIST OF MASKS

MASKS	COVERING
Happy Face	Sadness
Chameleon	Rejection
Strong	Vulnerability or Neediness
Bitch	Softness
Independent	Involvement
Workaholic	Feeling pain
Super Angry	Being hurt
Know-it-all	Inadequate
Intellectual	Foolishness
Helper	Hides one's own needs
Perfectionist	Being human
"I'm fine"	Being openly needy
People Pleaser	Rejection
Sarcastic Joker	Owning genuine feelings
Low Self-Esteem	Accepting greater challenge
Confused	May be avoiding the obvious
Judgmental	Rejection
Quiet	Fear or anger
Depressed	May be avoiding anger
Can't Trust the Opposite Sex	Mistrusts self
Poor Me	Responsibility
Caretaker	Own vulnerability
Martyr	Accountability
Aloof	Fear of involvement
Macho	Weakness
Runner	Failure

LIST OF MANIPULATIONS

- Posturing
- Respond w/query
- Feigning ignorance
- Abandonment
- Gaslighting
- Text instead of call
- Depression
- Lecturing
- Sickness
- Misrepresenting
- Us vs. them
- Flattery
- "Selling"
- Distorting
- Whining
- Shaming
- Forgetting
- Aggressing
- Expectations
- Repression
- Seduction
- Withdrawal
- Cynicism
- Always being helpful
- Cajoling
- Fear
- Suppression
- Blaming the victim
- Exploitative
- Submission
- Bullying

- Disorganized
- Anger
- Deceptive
- Neglect
- Sarcasm
- Excuses
- Name-calling
- Lying
- Baiting
- Affirmations
- Controlling
- Masking
- Overwhelm
- Avoidance
- Deflecting
- Very subdued
- Rejection
- Begging
- Always/never
- Contempt
- Devious
- Roleplaying
- Teasing
- Being very loud
- Denial
- Helplessness
- Triangulating
- Guilting
- Making promises to change
- I'm sorry, I'm sorry.....I'm sorry

- "Acting"
- Chaotic
- Pleading
- Justify
- Two-faced
- Rationalize
- Distrustful
- Abusive
- Silence
- "You think you have it bad...let me tell you what happened to me"
- Blackmail
- Numbing
- Constant victim
- Milquetoast
- Misdirecting
- With-holding
- Taking complete responsibility
- Taking no responsibility
- One-upmanship
- Despair
- Always "yes"
- Gossiping
- Threatening
- Poor nutrition/exercise
- Resentment
- Insincerity
- Suffering

Self-Worth vs Self-Esteem vs Self-Compassion

Self-worth, self-esteem, and self-compassion are closely related concepts, each playing a crucial role in one's overall well-being, yet they have distinct definitions and nuances. Understanding these differences can help individuals cultivate a healthier and more balanced sense of self.

Self-Worth is the fundamental belief that one has inherent value and deserves respect and love simply for being human. It is an intrinsic sense of worthiness that is not contingent on external achievements or validation. Self-worth is about recognizing your inherent dignity and value, regardless of circumstances or outcomes. It is the foundation upon which self-esteem is built, and it remains constant even in the face of failure or criticism.

Self-Esteem refers to the overall subjective evaluation of one's own worth. It encompasses how you perceive your abilities, achievements, and personal qualities. Self-esteem is often influenced by external factors such as success, approval from others, and social comparisons. High self-esteem means having a positive view of yourself and feeling competent and worthy of respect, while low self-esteem can lead to feelings of inadequacy and self-doubt. Unlike self-worth, self-esteem can fluctuate based on experiences and external feedback.

Self-Compassion involves treating yourself with the same kindness, understanding, and empathy that one would offer to a friend facing difficulties. It is about recognizing that imperfection and suffering are part of the shared human experience and responding to your mistakes and failures with gentleness rather than harsh criticism. Self-compassion includes three main components: self-kindness, common humanity, and mindfulness. It helps individuals maintain emotional resilience and a balanced perspective during tough times.

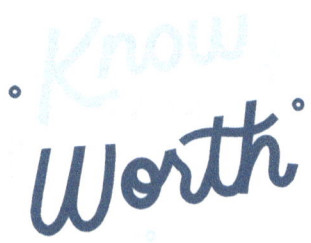

Self Worth Score _____

Social Self Worth Score _____

In terms of the Fisher Divorce Adjustment Survey (the "self-test") we define self worth as "what you say about yourself when you are alone". Social Self Worth is "what you say about yourself when you are with others".

Marriage Autopsy - Interactions

How did you let your partner know you were angry?
How did they let you know they were angry?
Did you deal with it directly, or did one of you hide it?
Did either of you try to hurt or get even with the other when angry? Explain.

Did you mutually agree on how you would share responsibilities for earning money and for household chores?
If not, how did that affect your relationship?

Did your partner show affection? Y/N
Did you get enough attention? Y/N
Did you get enough touching, hugs, compliments, sex, gifts, etc.? Y/N
Did your partner ever complain that they didn't get enough from you? Y/N
Did your partner complain about having to give attention or affection
to you? Y/N
Explain how any of these affected you or the relationship.

Did your partner try to shame, preach, moralize or change your feelings or
thoughts in any way that let you know that they didn't think your feelings or
thoughts were valid?
Did you ever do that to him or her?

Were you equals in all decision making and responsibilities or was one of you
more of a parent or child than a partner?
If you answered yes to the latter, how did that make you feel?

Esteeming Practices

Often people make the mistake of trying to do too much or go too big with their goals. Do only what you can handle and do consistently. The goal is not to get it all figured out. Self Esteem is something that takes time. Here are some ways to build your self esteem.

◆ **Esteem yourself in the mirror:** Go to the mirror and really look at yourself. Naked is best. Spend 5 minutes really looking at yourself. Learn to fall in love with what you see. Tell yourself about the things that you like about yourself.

◆ **Practice Honesty:** Be honest with yourself to develop trust in yourself. It doesn't have to be big. But do it. Where have you been lying to yourself? To others?

◆ **Practice Gratitude:** Every day write down 3 things you are grateful for. Notice how you feel when you write them down.

◆ **Sit in a room, any room for 15 minutes.** Look at every object in the room. How can you be grateful for it? How has it contributed to your life? It has a history. It is more than some people have.

◆ **Say "How can I give my best to life today?"** Identify where in your life you have high and low self esteem. Maybe work is high, but parenting is low. Or relationships are low. Choose the smallest step you can to step into growing your self esteem in the areas you feel low. Body image? What one small thing can you do every day?

◆ **De-shame yourself.** Shame is emotional quicksand. You can't get out alone. You need to share what you are ashamed of with others in order to get out of it. This is the secret. So tell someone something you are ashamed of.

◆ **Express your feelings If you are angry,** look for the unmet needs. What is going on? Look at your feelings and get clear about what you feel and why. If you need to express something then do it through journal/meditation, exercise, talking, etc.

◆ **Have a new consciousness:** Repeat to yourself: "I am enough. I am a gem. I am perfectly me. I am a beautiful person."

- ◆ **Move the legal process forward** If there are actions that you can take to move the legal process forward then do it this week.

- ◆ **Create or strengthen friendships:** Call a friend and say hello. Go meet them for a walk, a drink, a concert

- ◆ **Say "What..." instead of "Why..."** "What's next?" "What do I want?" instead of "Why do I..."

- ◆ **Change your home:** Paint a wall, move some furniture, put up new pictures. Make your home YOURS.

- ◆ **Plan your future** When are you going to achieve/do certain goals or activities?

- ◆ **Have a relationship ending ritual:** Create and perform a ceremony to let go of the relationship.

- ◆ **Decide on a respectful name for your ex** Some people don't like "my Ex". They prefer "The mother /father of my children" or "previous partner", or "The Ex". Some people give them names: The Panama man. A former friend.

- ◆ Tell others that you are divorcing. Be direct. Be honest. Say what is true and is happening. Notice what comes up for you, if anything.

- ◆ **Plan your next holiday** The first year after a split is the "year of firsts." The first birthday separated, the first New Year's Eve, the first family get together that you both don't attend. These are difficult times. So plan them out ahead of time. How can you get through it gracefully, powerfully, and authentically?

- ◆ **Don't compare:** Practice not comparing yourself to anyone else. Comparison is the thief of joy. Positively or negatively.

- ◆ **Create mantras or affirmations Self Affirmations** - Be specific, be clear, be accurate.

- ◆ **Be authentic in your communication.** It makes you feel more alive. ("That really hurt me." "That affected me.")

- ◆ **Practice Appreciation:** Show appreciation for others or for yourself : "that was a really nice thing you did"

- **Practice receiving or taking in compliments**

- **Tell yourself "I CAN..."** Practice "I can do this" instead of "I can't do this"

- **Practice Self Compassion** Give yourself a break. Be a friend to you. Be understanding. Let yourself off the hook.

- **Appreciate Yourself** Acknowledge all that you do for you. All that you have done. Write it down.

- **Do something you have always wanted to do** It is your time. There is no other life for you to do it in. Now is the time to start living for you instead of others. So what is something you have always wanted to do? Plan it or do it.

- **Be your own best friend.** Give yourself the advice you would give to a friend. Listen to yourself. Treat yourself the way you would treat a friend.

- **Ask yourself "What do I GET to do?"** Instead of "What do I have to do?" Recognize your talents. What are you particularly good at? Use it. Share it. Do it. Try it again. Practice it.

- **Say to yourself "I MATTER"** What you mutter MATTERS. Right when you wake up in the morning say "I MATTER".

- **Do basic hygiene:** Shower, nails, hair, shave, dress nice. Sometimes the basics are enough

- **Get Support** Reach out to a friend, therapist, counselor, family for support

- **Ask your friends to listen.** Tell a friend that you just need to talk to someone that can listen. No advice, no judgment, just understanding.

- **Have a Vision** What do you want your life to look like? Imagine it without obstacles. What is a vision of your next chapter of this life?

- **Prayer and Meditation** Pray, meditate, reflect. Quiet your mind.

- **Re-Image Yourself. What does the "New You" want?** What does the "New You" need? What is the price you are paying to not accept yourself? To understand your sense of well being?

The Emotional Ladder

How do you climb a ladder? One step at a time!

People often want to feel happy instead of what they are feeling, like anger and sadness. They tell themselves that they need to ignore those other feelings. We use the idea of the emotional ladder as a way to convey a very important concept. If you want to treat yourself better, don't expect to suddenly get to the "top" emotions. Instead aim for the next rung on the ladder.

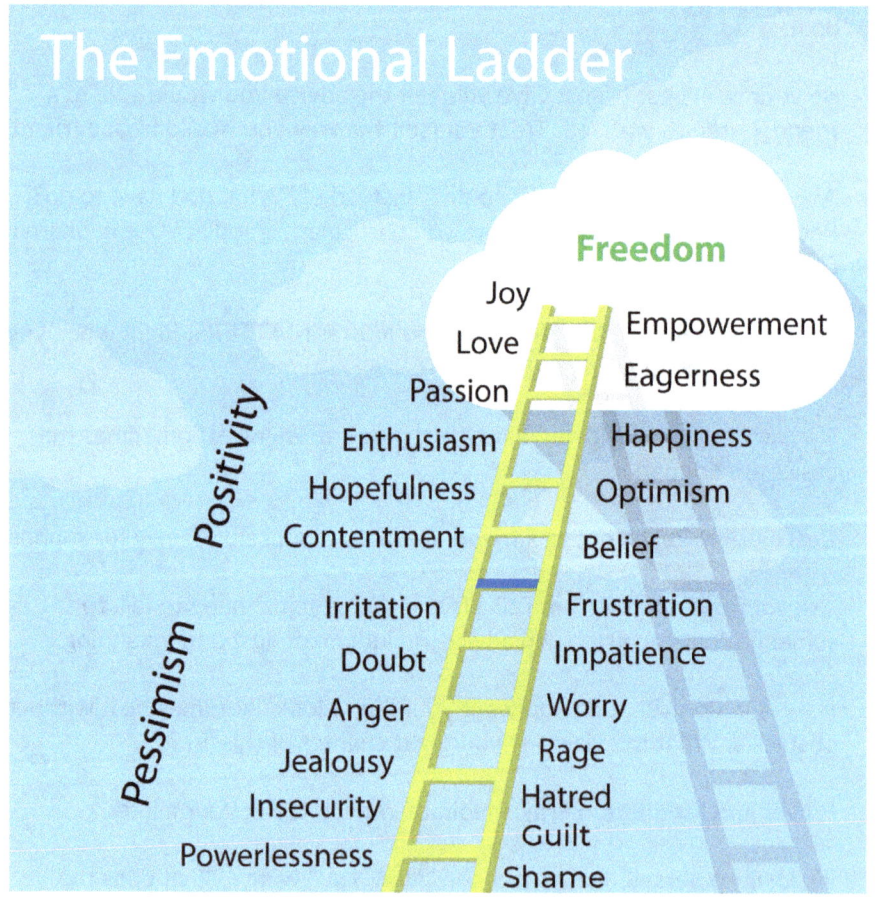

The Emotional Ladder

Freedom

Joy
Love
Passion
Enthusiasm
Hopefulness
Contentment

Empowerment
Eagerness
Happiness
Optimism
Belief

Positivity

Irritation
Doubt
Anger
Jealousy
Insecurity
Powerlessness

Frustration
Impatience
Worry
Rage
Hatred
Guilt
Shame

Pessimism

BLOCKS TO INTIMACY

- Martyr
- Victim
- Sickness
- Guilt
- Fighting
- Sex
- Violating Boundaries
- Withdrawing or quietness
- Make everything a growth issue
- Controlling
- Manipulation
- Fear:
  - of loss of self
  - of being vulnerable
  - of inadequacy
  - of abandonment
  - of rejection or criticism
  - of having intimacy used against you
  - of repeating dysfunctional relationship
  - of having boundaries violated
  - of loss
  - of competition
  - of avoidance
  - of other person's anger
- Preconceived limits
- Lack of boundaries
- Dependency/Co-dependency
- Lack of emotional space
- Rebellion
- Masks
- Sexuality (using sex as power)
- Expectations
- Inflexibility
- Chameleon
- Poor personal hygiene (showering/oral hygiene)

- Using substance to numb or reduce inhibition
- False promises
- Sarcasm
- Teasing
- Humor
- "Push-Pull"-emotionally
- Long distance relationship
- Caretaking
- Being nice/people-pleasing
- Provoking conflict
- Not knowing your wants & needs
- Don't believe intimacy is possible
- Inability to express anger
- Low self-esteem
- False assumptions
- Judgments
- Criticism
- Dishonesty
- Untrustworthy
- Belief systems (self-limiting)
- Need to be "right"
- Losing self for the other
- Humor to avoid intimacy
- Jealousy
- Shame of self or shaming other
- Lack of respect
- Lack of awareness
- Defensiveness
- Unresolved guilt
- Playing psychological games
- Abuse
- Acting righteously
- Abandonment
- Rejection
- Lying
- Blaming
- Sarcasm
- Condemning
- Perfectionist

- Indirect communication
- Letting anger build & exploding
- Maladaptive behaviors
- Domination
- Lack of self-responsibility
- Secrets
- Rejecting other or making them
- feel guilty
- Jealousy
- Withholding – emotionally
- Playing an inauthentic role
- Acting defensively
- Belief in scarcity
- Lack of commitment
- Filling your life with busyness
- Taking each other for granted
- Acting controlling
- Mind reading:
  - expecting others to know what you want or need
  - assuming what others want or need
- Being parental
- Learned childhood reactions
- Projection
- Fighting
- Vying for victim position
- Denial of feelings
- Not telling truth
- Arguments
- Illness or disease from not expressing ones needs or emotions.
- Competition
- Idealism
- Childhood issues unresolved
- Failure beliefs about self or others
- Procrastination
- Name calling

Intimacy with Self

- Nurturing self
- Honesty
- Tuning into your body
- Humor - laugh at & with self
- Forgiving ourselves & others
- Finding balance in yourself
- Journaling
- Self-encounters
- Risking
- Gentleness towards self & others
- Talking with others
- Taking responsibility for self
- Using "I" messages
- Feel your feelings
- Staying in present
- Time alone and with self
- Introspection
- Breathing
- Music
- Awareness
- Remember to play
- Personal growth
- Gentle nurturing of yourself
- Ownership of behavior/emotions & needs
- Ability to soothe & comfort
- Honesty (authentic)
- Staying current
- Relaxation & recreation
- Exercise (acceptance of body)
- Spirituality
- Boundaries
- Expressing feelings
- Management of feelings
- Trust in yourself
- Sharing self & feelings
- Fulfilling dreams/purpose
- Speak up for self-truth
- Patience
- Notice your self-talk
- Positive affirmations
- Authority over inner judge & critic
- Choosing to love yourself
- Expressing love
- Meeting the needs only you can fulfill

Intimacy with Others

- Warmth
- Serenity
- Fun & joy
- Sharing freely with each other
- Acceptance of each other
- Intention to be intimate
- Willingness to be known
- Feeling safe
- Active listening
- Encouragement
- Being emotionally open
- Understanding
- Expressing fears
- Honoring one another
- Become intimate with self first
- Being vulnerable
- Sharing my boundaries
- Being truthful
- Sincere caring
- "Walk your talk"
- Nurturing
- Receiving (openness)
- Hugging
- Kissing
- Appropriate touch
- Patience
- Individuality
- Honoring boundaries
- Sharing my emotional pain
- Being responsible for self
- Risking
- Being together and being able to
- be separate
- Validating
- Empathy
- Spending quality time
- Not advising or trying to fix
- Non-parental
- Expressing & accepting
- Feelings
- Communication
- No criticism
- Mutuality
- Gifts
- Spiritual growth
- Gentleness
- Trust
- Romance
- Self-knowledge
- Commitment
- Honoring other person
- Respect
- Inner child connectedness
- Affirmations
- Freedom to be yourself
- Expressing wants & needs
- Really listening
- "I" messages – "I feel" ...
- Asking for wants & needs
- Responsible for self
- Cooperation
- Balance
- Direct eye contact
- Friendship
- Honesty
- Having fun
- Living in the moment
- Dealing with issues/resolution
- Allowing emotional space
- Timing
- Talking about sexual needs
- Similar values/beliefs
- Like the other person
- Bringing out the best in someone
- Unconditional love
- Sharing self & feelings
- Sharing blocks to intimacy
- Healing encounters
- Self encounters
- Cleaning "emotional windshield"
- Being supportive
- Letting go of expectations

Marriage Autopsy - Intimacy

What were the most common and recurring arguments that you had?

Did you agree on the methods for solving problems between you? (not necessarily the solutions but the method for problem solving?) Explain.

Did you make major decisions jointly? Did you consider the effects of your decisions on one another? YES / NO. If not, explain how this affected you.

Could you each share your innermost thoughts about life, goals, challenges, needs, fears, sex, health, likes and dislikes? YES/NO. If not, explain how that affected you

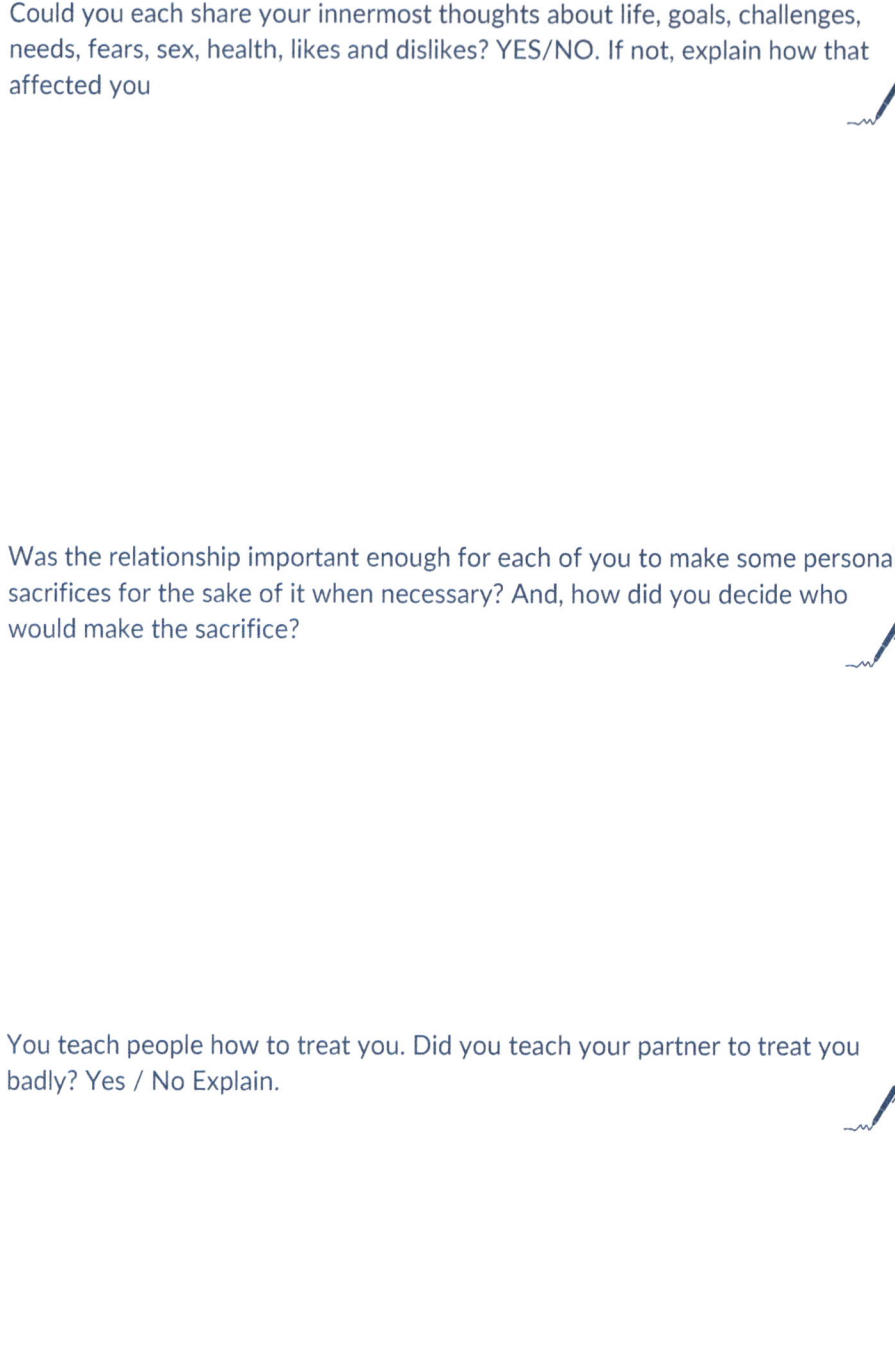

Was the relationship important enough for each of you to make some personal sacrifices for the sake of it when necessary? And, how did you decide who would make the sacrifice?

You teach people how to treat you. Did you teach your partner to treat you badly? Yes / No Explain.

Love

What did you learn as a child about love?

What did I learn as an adolescent about love?

What did I learn as a young adult about love?

Write a definition of your old adult love relationship.

What are your 5 Love Language results? (Rebuilders.net/5lovelangs)

1. _____

2. _____

3. _____

4. _____

5. _____

What do you love?

Ten things you LOVE about yourself:

1. _____
2. _____
3. _____
4. _____
5. _____
6. _____
7. _____
8. _____
9. _____
10. _____

Five things you appreciate about yourself:

1. _____
2. _____
3. _____
4. _____
5. _____

If you love your life how would you know? What would you be doing?

What are you going to do this coming week to love yourself?

Self-Compassion

Kristen Neff is a researcher that has done a lot of investigation into Self Worth, Self Esteem, and Self Compassion. Her research shows that Self Compassion can do more for people than anything else.

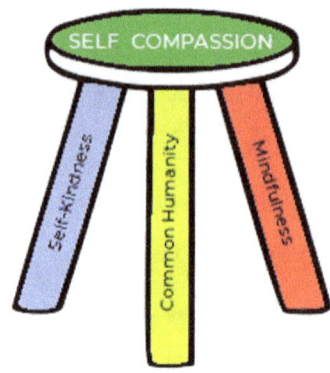

She has found that there are three "legs" of Self Compassion:

- ☐ **Self-Kindness:** Being caring towards ourselves
- ☐ **Common Humanity:** A sense of interconnectedness. Pain is part of the shared human experience.
- ☐ **Mindfulness:** Being aware of moment-to-moment experience in a clear and balanced manner.

How kind are you towards yourself?

Mindfulness

Mindfulness is the practice of being fully present and engaged in the current moment, aware of your thoughts, feelings, and sensations without judgment. It involves observing your experiences with openness and curiosity, allowing you to respond to situations with greater clarity and calmness. Mindfulness can improve emotional regulation, reduce stress, and enhance overall well-being.

Proven Techniques to Improve Mindfulness

◆ **Mindful Breathing:** Focus on your breath, observing the inhalation and exhalation. Notice the sensation of the air entering and leaving your body. If your mind wanders, gently bring your attention back to your breath.

◆ **Body Scan Meditation:** Gradually focus on different parts of your body, starting from your toes and moving up to your head. Notice any sensations, tension, or relaxation in each area.

◆ **Mindful Walking:** Pay attention to the sensation of your feet touching the ground, the movement of your legs, and the rhythm of your steps. Be aware of your surroundings, noticing sights, sounds, and smells.

◆ **Mindful Eating:** Eat slowly and savor each bite. Notice the taste, texture, and aroma of your food. Pay attention to the sensations in your mouth and how your body feels as you eat.

◆ **Mindfulness Meditation:** Set aside time each day to sit quietly and meditate. Focus on your breath, a mantra, or a specific sensation. When your mind wanders, gently redirect your attention back to your focus.

◆ **Mindful Listening:** When interacting with others, listen fully without planning your response while they are speaking. Pay attention to their words, tone, and body language.

◆ **Gratitude Practice:** Take time each day to reflect on things you are grateful for. Write them down in a journal or simply think about them. This practice can shift your focus to positive aspects of your life.

◆ **Yoga and Tai Chi:** These practices combine physical movement with mindfulness, helping you become more aware of your body and breath. They can reduce stress and improve mental clarity.

◆ **Mindful Journaling:** Write about your thoughts and feelings without judgment. This practice can help you process emotions and gain insights into your experiences.

◆ **Mindful Observation:** Choose an object in your environment and observe it closely. Notice its shape, color, texture, and any other details. This practice can help you develop a deeper appreciation for the present moment.

Benefits of Mindfulness

◆ **Reduces Stress:** Mindfulness helps lower cortisol levels, reducing stress and anxiety.

◆ **Improves Emotional Regulation:** It enhances your ability to manage emotions, leading to better emotional stability.

◆ **Enhances Focus and Concentration:** Regular practice can improve your attention span and cognitive function.

◆ **Promotes Better Sleep:** Mindfulness practices can help calm your mind, leading to improved sleep quality.

◆ **Boosts Overall Well-being:** It fosters a greater sense of happiness, contentment, and overall life satisfaction.

Getting Started

Start with small, manageable practices and gradually increase the duration and frequency. Consistency is key to experiencing the benefits of mindfulness. Consider joining a mindfulness group or using apps and online resources to support your practice.

Relationships

People in committed relationships often live longer and happier lives, supported by numerous studies highlighting the benefits of companionship and emotional support. However, for those who have experienced the pain of divorce, the thought of entering a new relationship can be daunting. The fear of repeating past heartbreaks is understandable, yet many still yearn for the safety and comfort of having a partner. The key to avoiding the repetition of past mistakes lies in making conscious changes and adopting new approaches to relationships.

To create a healthier and more fulfilling relationship, it is crucial to learn essential skills that foster growth and intimacy. These skills can help transform a relationship from one of disconnection and dissatisfaction to one of connection and contentment. In the following pages, we will provide you with various tools and information designed to guide you on this journey. By embracing these resources, you can build a stronger foundation for your future relationships and navigate the complexities of love with confidence and resilience.

> **When are you ready to date again? When you are ready to be hurt again**

Are you ready to date again? (REALLY ready?)

Social Trust Score _____

You can check this by looking at your Social Trust score. If it is less than 80 then there are probably things you need to work on BEFORE you get into the next relationship.

Singleness

Embracing singleness after a divorce can be an incredibly daunting journey. Many of us fear the prospect of being alone, feeling as though we have lost a crucial part of our identity or security. However, this period of singleness is not just a void to be filled; it is a profound opportunity for self-discovery and growth. Facing the challenge of being alone head-on allows us to heal, understand our true selves, and redefine our values and desires. This evolution is crucial for developing a healthy, independent mindset that is not reliant on another person for fulfillment.

When we learn to be comfortable and content in our own company, we liberate ourselves from entering relationships out of fear or desperation. Instead, we approach new relationships with a sense of confidence and clear boundaries, ensuring that we do not tolerate the negative behaviors of the past. This self-assuredness makes us better partners, as we hold ourselves and our partners to higher standards. Ultimately, this strengthens the relationship, fostering mutual respect and understanding. By mastering the art of being alone, we lay the foundation for healthier, more fulfilling relationships in the future.

Reflect on Your Fears: What are your biggest fears about being single? How do these fears impact your daily life and your view of relationships? Write about where these fears may have originated and what steps you can take to address and overcome them.

Embracing Solitude: Describe a time when you felt truly content being alone. What activities, thoughts, or feelings contributed to that sense of peace? How can you incorporate more of these moments into your life to better embrace your singleness?

Defining Your Standards: What qualities do you value most in yourself and in a partner? How can being single help you reinforce and maintain these standards? Reflect on how having clear boundaries and self-respect can enhance your future relationships.

The Four Horsemen of Divorce

And how to stop them with their antidotes

Although many of us believe that anger is the root cause of unhappy relationships, John Gottman notes that it is not conflict itself that is the problem, but how we handle it. Venting anger constructively can actually do wonders to clear the air and get a relationship back in balance. However, conflict does become a problem when it is characterized by the presence of what Gottman calls the "Four Horsemen of the Apocalypse".

Horseman	Antidote
Criticism: Verbally attacking personality or character	**Gentle Start Up:** Talk about your feelings using "I" statements and express a positive need.
Contempt: Attacking sense of self with an intent to insult or abuse	**Build Culture of Appreciation:** Remind yourself of your partner's positive qualities and find gratitude for positive actions.
Defensiveness: Victimizing yourself to ward off a perceived attach and reverse the blame	**Take Responsibility:** Accept your partner's perspective and offer an apology for any wrongdoing.
Stonewalling: Withdrawing to avoid conflict and convey disapproval, distance, and separation.	**Physiological Self Soothing:** Take a break and spend that time doing something soothing and distracting.

Which of the Horseman are/were in your relationship? Explain

Codependency Part 2

Codependency is a behavioral condition where one person enables another person's addiction, poor mental health, immaturity, irresponsibility, or under-achievement. It often involves excessive emotional or psychological reliance on a partner, typically one who requires support due to an illness or addiction. Codependent relationships are characterized by a lack of boundaries, a tendency to take on the other person's problems as one's own, and an unhealthy balance where one person's needs and desires dominate the relationship.

Codependency	Interdependency
Excessive Caretaking:	Balanced Caregiving
Low Self Esteem	High Self Esteem
People-Pleasing	Supportive
Poor Boundaries	Healthy Boundaries
Reactivity	Responsiveness
Control Issues	Mutual Respect
Dysfunctional Communication	Healthy Communication
Obsession with Relationships	Self Awareness

The Alternative to Codependency is developing healthy interdependence. Interdependence involves mutual support and respect between partners, where each individual maintains their own identity and independence while also being emotionally connected and supportive.

Circle the characteristics of codependency that you recognize in your relationship (yours or your partners) in the list above

Forgiveness

Everything that relates to forgiveness has happened. What is occurring today is in your mind. Reflect on what it would be like to be free of the negative thoughts and feelings - hostility, resentment, hate etc.

What would you gain if you could let go of these feelings and change your thinking?

The three aspects of forgiveness are:
forgiving others
forgiving yourself and
asking for forgiveness.

Most people focus on the first. Some on the second , rarely on the third. What changes in thinking and feelings would you have to make to be able to forgive or ask for forgiveness?

Einstein said "You cannot solve a problem in the same consciousness in which it was created". Which consciousness will enable you to create peace within yourself and peace with the persons(s) that you are in conflict with?

Communication

Communication is fundamental to a healthy relationship. When things are going well, it feels natural and effortless. However, when a relationship faces distress or conflict, communication becomes more challenging yet more crucial. Ironically, conflict is the perfect time to communicate, but it often leads to greater disconnection. Many people mistakenly think that if their partner doesn't understand them, it might mean they shouldn't be together. In reality, both partners usually want to be understood and to understand each other. They crave love, support, and acceptance. What they often lack are the tools and guidance to transform conflicts into opportunities for growth and connection.

To address this, we turn to the remarkable work of Dr. Marshall Rosenberg and his approach known as Non-Violent Communication (NVC). Despite its unusual name, NVC is a powerful framework that aligns closely with the skills and concepts we've explored in this workbook. NVC offers a practical roadmap for improving relationships, especially during conflicts. It teaches us how to express our needs and feelings without blame, and how to listen with empathy, fostering deeper understanding and connection. To learn more about NVC and how we incorporate it into our work, visit Dr. Rosenberg's website and continue with the exercises and strategies outlined in this workbook.

Reflect on a time during your relationship when conflict led to disconnection. What were the main points of misunderstanding, and how did you and your partner attempt to communicate?

Think about a moment when you felt truly understood and supported by your partner. What was the communication like in that situation?

Identify a specific conflict or communication breakdown that contributed to the end of your relationship. Write it in detail here (you will use this later):

Non-Violent Communication

Non-Violent Communication (NVC), developed by Dr. Marshall Rosenberg, is a communication framework designed to foster empathy, understanding, and peaceful conflict resolution. NVC emphasizes expressing one's feelings and needs honestly while also actively listening to understand others' perspectives without judgment. The process involves four key components: making objective observations, identifying and expressing feelings, understanding and articulating underlying needs, and making clear, actionable requests. By focusing on these elements, NVC helps individuals connect more deeply, resolve conflicts constructively, and build mutually satisfying relationships. This approach is widely used in various contexts, from personal relationships to professional environments, and has proven effective in enhancing communication and fostering empathy.

Observations

The first step in Non-Violent Communication (NVC) is making observations. Observations involve objectively describing what we see or hear without adding interpretations, judgments, or evaluations. This clarity helps avoid misunderstandings and defensiveness, creating a foundation for constructive dialogue. Differentiating observations from evaluations is crucial: an observation is a neutral statement of fact, while an evaluation includes our subjective interpretations or judgments. For example, saying "You interrupted me twice during dinner" is an observation, whereas "You were rude during dinner" is an evaluation. By focusing on clear observations, we can communicate more effectively and minimize conflict.

Evaluation	Observations
You are lazy.	You haven't completed the chores you agreed to do this week.
You were aggressive	You raised your voice and clenched your fists during our conversation.
You were disrespectful.	You walked away while I was still talking.
You are insensitive.	You laughed when I shared my concerns.

What specific actions or words did I observe in the situation (in your original reflection) without adding my interpretation or judgment?

How might my initial evaluations of these actions or words have influenced my feelings and reactions during the conflict?

Feelings

The second step in Non-Violent Communication (NVC) involves identifying and expressing feelings. This step is about accurately recognizing and articulating our emotional responses to specific situations. By clearly stating our feelings, we help others understand our internal experiences, paving the way for empathy and connection. It's essential to differentiate between actual feelings and thoughts or interpretations disguised as feelings. True feelings are emotional states like sadness, joy, anger, or fear, whereas thoughts are our interpretations or judgments about the situation. For example, saying "I feel ignored" is often a thought about someone else's behavior, while "I feel lonely" accurately expresses an emotional state.

What specific emotions did I experience during the conflict, and how can I describe these feelings accurately? (Look at the Feelings Compass on page 63)

How did my thoughts or interpretations of the other person's actions influence my feelings in this situation?

Needs

The third step in Non-Violent Communication (NVC) focuses on identifying and articulating our needs. Needs are the fundamental drivers behind our feelings and actions, representing what is essential for our well-being and fulfillment. Recognizing and clearly expressing our needs helps others understand what truly matters to us, creating a basis for resolving conflicts and fostering mutual support. It's crucial to connect our feelings to these unmet or met needs, as emotions often signal whether our needs are being satisfied or not. For example, feeling frustrated might indicate an unmet need for respect or understanding, while feeling joyful might reflect a fulfilled need for connection or appreciation.

What specific needs were unmet or met during the conflict, and how did these needs influence my feelings? (Reference the Needs Map on page 107)

How can I clearly articulate my needs in future interactions to better address and resolve conflicts?

Requests

The fourth step in Non-Violent Communication (NVC) involves formulating clear, specific, and actionable requests. This step is about expressing what we want from others in a way that is respectful and doable, aiming to meet our needs without coercion. Effective requests are concrete and precise, specifying what actions would help address our needs. It's crucial to distinguish between requests and demands: a request invites collaboration and leaves room for the other person to say no or suggest alternatives, while a demand implies an expectation of compliance and can lead to resistance or resentment. For instance, "Could you please listen to me for five minutes without interrupting?" is a request, whereas "You need to stop interrupting me right now" sounds more like a demand (tone matters too!).

What specific requests did I make during the conflict, and how clear and actionable were they?

In reflecting on my interactions, did I make a request and were there moments where my requests may have come across as demands?

How can I rephrase them as genuine requests in the future?

Boundaries

Boundaries are essential for healthy relationships. They protect your well-being and ensure mutual respect. This section will help you identify, set, and maintain boundaries effectively. People often give up on themselves in order to save a relationship. Ironically, setting boundaries can improve and even save a relationship.

What are boundaries?
Boundaries are limits you set to protect your personal space, emotions, and time.

Types of Boundaries:
- Physical
- Emotional
- Mental
- Digital
- Material

Boundaries foster respect, reduce stress, and enhance relationship quality.

Boundaries are not emotional, they are simply identifying where the "line" is. Boundaries are not for one person, they should apply to anyone.

How to Identify Your Boundaries:
- Self-Reflection: Think about past experiences where your boundaries were respected or violated.
- Core Needs and Values: Identify what is non-negotiable for your well-being.
- Signs of Overstepping: Notice when you feel uncomfortable, disrespected, or stressed.

How to Set Boundaries:
- Communication: Clearly express your boundaries to your partner.
- Practical Steps: Use "I" statements, be specific, and stay firm but kind.
- Examples: "I need time alone after work to recharge."

How to Enforce Your Boundaries:
- Consistency: Stick to your boundaries even when it's challenging.
- Dealing with Pushback: Calmly restate your boundaries and the reasons behind them.
- Reevaluation: Regularly review and adjust your boundaries as needed.

Examples of Boundaries

 Physical
- I need at least one night to myself (alone) each week.
- No one meets my kids for 6 months
- No physical intimacy for 6 weeks.

 Emotional:
- If I am not ready to talk about something and I tell you that, I need you to respect that.
- If I am not happy, you don't need to fix me or help me. I can work through it myself. If there is something you can do I will let you know.

 Mental:
- My values and beliefs are mine and are not negotiable. These are what make me unique. I am happy to share them with you but I ask that you not try to change them or judge them.
- I have things that trigger me. I am working through those things. I am not okay with you intentionally trying to trigger me or use them against me.

 Digital:
- What I do on my cell phone is private. I do not have to share with you my conversations, my location, or what I do with it.
- What I share with you in texts or in photos is private, between us. I do not give you permission to share it with others.

 Material:
- If I let you borrow something that is mine, I expect you to take care of it and return it in the same condition that I lent it to you.
- If you are in my home, I ask that you honor that this is my space and that you allow me to be comfortable in it, however I want it to look.

Describe a time when your boundaries were respected. How did it make you feel?

Describe a time when your boundaries were violated. What was the impact on you?

How can I rephrase them as genuine requests in the future?

Identify at least three boundaries for you:

1. ————————————————————————————
2. ————————————————————————————
3. ————————————————————————————

How can you communicate these boundaries clearly and respectfully?

What challenges do you anticipate in maintaining your boundaries?

How can you stay consistent in upholding your boundaries?

Marriage Autopsy - Strengths and Weaknesses

What were each of your strengths? Did each of you support each other's strengths?
Did you see the other person's weaknesses in the beginning only to deny them and then later become invested in trying to change them? Explain.

Write down the problems your partner had with you. What did they complain about the most? Be honest with yourself as this may be a gift for a future relationship. If you recognize the complaints as an honest part of your character that needs to change you could work on that while you are still single.

Cause of Death - Did internal issues such as lack of time together, disrespect, loyalty with others over loyalty with each other etc. make the relationship susceptible to external influences such as affairs, work-a-holism, getting over-involved with activities etc.?
If so, what were those issues?
Was there any possibility of resuscitation between the time of death and notification?
Identify the root causes of why the relationship began to suffer and then eventually died.

Write down 10 key statements about the pain you still feel and the open wounds you still have. Again, honesty is essential.

Attachment Styles

Attachment styles are psychological patterns that describe how individuals form and maintain emotional bonds with others. Originating from the work of John Bowlby and Mary Ainsworth, these styles are primarily shaped during childhood through interactions with primary caregivers. The way caregivers respond to a child's needs can lead to the development of secure or insecure attachment styles. A secure attachment forms when caregivers are consistently responsive and supportive, fostering a sense of safety and trust in the child. On the other hand, inconsistent, neglectful, or overly intrusive caregiving can result in insecure attachment styles, such as anxious, avoidant, or disorganized attachment.

Understanding attachment styles is crucial because they significantly influence how individuals relate to others in adulthood, particularly in romantic relationships. Those with a secure attachment style typically feel comfortable with intimacy and are able to maintain healthy, balanced relationships. Conversely, individuals with insecure attachment styles may struggle with emotional regulation, fear of abandonment, or intimacy issues. For instance, people with an anxious attachment style may crave closeness yet fear rejection, while those with an avoidant attachment style might distance themselves to avoid vulnerability. Recognizing and understanding one's attachment style can be a vital step towards personal growth and improving relationship dynamics.

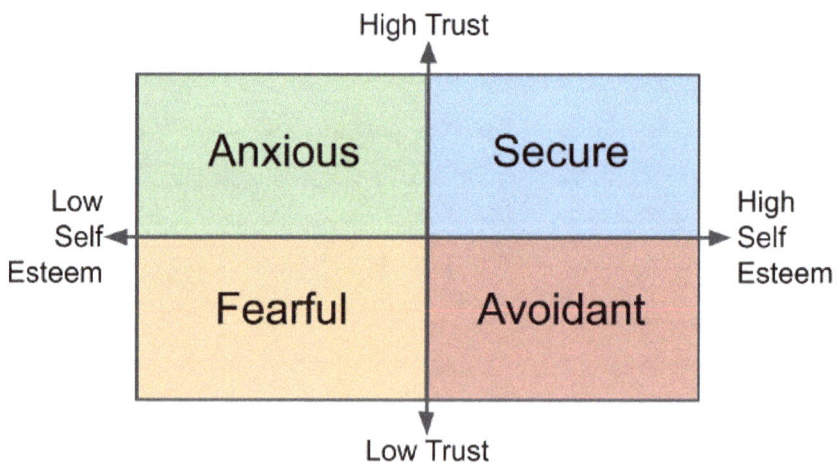

Anxious attachment style

Anxious attachment style, characterized by high trust in others but low self-esteem, often leads to a heightened fear of abandonment and a deep-seated fear of being alone. Individuals with this attachment style tend to be preoccupied with their relationships, frequently seeking reassurance and validation from their partners. This preoccupation can result in codependent behaviors, where they may prioritize their partner's needs over their own to maintain the relationship. When faced with perceived threats to their relationship, they might respond with a fawn or freeze reaction, either by excessively pleasing their partner to avoid conflict or by becoming emotionally paralyzed.

Fearful attachment style

The **Fearful attachment style** is marked by low trust in others and low self-esteem, creating a complex and often tumultuous approach to relationships. Individuals with this attachment style experience a push-pull dynamic, where they simultaneously crave intimacy and fear it, leading to confusing and contradictory behaviors. Their response to relationship triggers can vary widely, reflecting their internal conflict and ambivalence about love. Often, they downplay the importance of relationships to protect themselves from potential hurt, yet struggle with feelings of loneliness and emotional disconnection. This attachment style also involves trouble with recognizing and expressing emotions, making it challenging for them to form deep, meaningful connections.

Avoidant attachment style

The **Avoidant attachment style** is characterized by low trust in others but high self-esteem, resulting in a tendency to distance oneself emotionally from relationships. Individuals with this style have difficulty trusting others and often respond to stressors with freeze or flight reactions. They build up emotional walls to protect themselves from potential hurt, fostering an ultra-independent persona that prioritizes self-sufficiency over connection. While they may appear dismissive and uninterested in relationships, they do desire intimacy but are afraid of vulnerability and the potential for rejection. This fear leads them to keep others at arm's length, avoiding deep emotional bonds to maintain a sense of control and safety.

Secure attachment style

Secure attachment style is characterized by high trust in others and high self-esteem, forming the foundation for healthy and balanced relationships. Individuals with the **Secure attachment style** are not easily triggered, and if they do encounter stressors, they are adept at managing their emotional responses. They can attune to their own emotions and the emotions of others, fostering empathy and understanding in their interactions. With a healthy view of themselves, they speak their wants and needs clearly and confidently, leading to effective communication and mutual respect in relationships. This strong sense of self-worth allows them to navigate relational challenges with resilience and maintain a positive outlook on both themselves and their connections with others. Understanding secure attachment provides a model for striving towards emotional well-being and fulfilling relationships.

What is your attachment style?

Can you see how your attachment style developed?

Can you see how you can become more aware of the influence of your "default" mode effects your relationships?

Recommended Resources:
Hold Me Tight by *Dr. Sue Johnson*
Wired for Love by *Stan Tatkin*

Intimacy

> "Into Me, I See"

Intimacy is a close, familiar, and usually affectionate or loving personal relationship with another person or group. It involves a deep connection and understanding, which can be emotional, physical, or intellectual.

1. **Emotional Intimacy:** Sharing personal feelings, thoughts, and experiences, fostering trust and mutual respect.
2. **Physical Intimacy:** Expressing affection through touch, such as hugging, kissing, or sexual activities.
3. **Intellectual Intimacy:** Sharing ideas, engaging in meaningful conversations, and connecting on a cognitive level.
4. **Spiritual Intimacy:** Sharing beliefs, values, and experiences related to spirituality or religion.

Intimacy is characterized by vulnerability, openness, and a strong sense of trust and safety between the involved parties. It plays a crucial role in developing and maintaining healthy, enduring relationships.

In this workbook we explore your thoughts, feelings, values and beliefs and more. This is a foundation for you learning who YOU are. When you can be vulnerable with someone and share who you REALLY are, there is intimacy.

We crave intimacy. To be known. To be understood. To matter. When we can share that with another, relationships are no longer transactional. They are magical.

Reflect on a Time of Emotional Intimacy: Think about a time when you shared your personal feelings, thoughts, or experiences with someone and felt truly understood and respected. What was the situation, and how did it make you feel?

What did you learn about yourself and the other person from this experience?

Intellectual and Spiritual Connections: Reflect on a relationship (whether real or imagined) in terms of intellectual and spiritual intimacy. How do you share your ideas, beliefs, and values with others?

Describe a meaningful conversation or experience that deepened your connection with someone on an intellectual or spiritual level. What impact did it have on your relationship?

Marriage Autopsy - Reflection

Your past relationship has given you many gifts. It has taught you what you did like about a partner and will need in a future relationship. What did you like about your partner or what was good about that time in your life that you hope to find again in a future relationship?

What were some things that were not good about your relationship which you will never tolerate again if you were to have a future relationship?

Name some things you needed from your partner but didn't get but you will insist on in a future relationship.

Name some things your partner did right that you are grateful for.

Healthy Relationships

When I Feel Responsible

For Others (UNHEALTHY)	To Others (HEALTHY)
I fix	I show empathy
I protect	I encourage
I rescue	I share
I control	I confront
I carry their feelings	I level with them
I don't listen	I listen
I am insensitive	I am sensitive
I feel tired	I feel relaxed
I feel anxious	I feel free
I feel fearful	I feel aware
I feel liable	I feel high self-esteem
I am concerned with:	I am concerned with:
The solution	Relating person to person
Answers	Feelings
Circumstance	The person
Being right	Discovering truth
Details	The big picture
performance	Relating
I am a manipulator	I am a helper guide.
I expect the person to live up to my expectations	I expect the person to be responsible for self.
I feel fearful and hang on.	I can trust and let go.

Who do you want to BE in a relationship? Describe it using the table above to identify characteristics and behaviors that you want to demonstrate.

Purpose

Now that you are in the divorce process (or are divorced), imagine what you can now do with your life. Since you no longer need your partner's approval for how to spend your time or money-what do you "get to do with your life"?

There is always some resistance to change. As you reimagine your life, what resistance do you have to creating a new purpose, a new job, a new career, moving to a new location to fulfill a new sense (or renewed) of purpose? It will be helpful to journal about this every day .

You were likely emotionally enmeshed and entangled in your relationship. Often, as we gain a new vision or sense of purpose, we can more easily let go and disentangle.
What support do you need to discover your purpose? To fulfill your purpose?

What vision for your future can you create that relates to passion, purpose, fulfillment and meaning?

How has my perspective on life changed since my divorce? How can I embrace these changes to help me find and live my true purpose?

Your Story Again

Congratulations on reaching the end of this workbook. Now that you have done some of the exercises and you are ready to start the new chapter of your life, **take a moment to rewrite your story** - the same one you started with. However, this time write it from authentic consciousness. Write it as an empowered, authentic and caring person that has reflected on what happened and is now ready to embrace a new life that is about to begin.

Journal Prompt 1

Looking back: How were you co-dependent in your relationship? How did you give your power away? Can you remember a time when you were truly happy? What contributed to your happiness then? **Looking forward:** Authentic Consciousness is foreign to most people. It's easier to think about how you could practice the following: Reminding yourself that you are "enough". How might you do that? Be vulnerable. Share with others what is really going on with you-what you are feeling, what you need, or how you have been affected- (with people that are accepting and close enough). Be assertive. How might you practice saying "I like this" or "I don't want to do that". You don't have to explain yourself. Where might you do that and with who? Be caring. How might you better care for YOURSELF? **Other:** What is the most courageous thing I have ever done? What hurt from my childhood that has never been healed?

Journal Prompt 2

People rarely say, "I really want to grieve my marriage." Usually they say, "I'm so sad." "I miss him or her." Then when we start talking about other losses in their life there are usually many more losses that haven't fully been grieved. The loss of parents, loss of children, loss of friends, THE LOSS OF TIME, The loss of childbearing years, loss of favorite pets, a great boss, a job that was amazing, a favorite car, a home, etc. Sometimes it is helpful to reflect on the things you have lost. What do you miss? Do you still miss them? How MUCH do you miss them? Think about things in your past that you haven't completely said good bye to. How do these events in your life compare to your divorce? More or less? Also, grief can be cumulative. We may have lots events that we haven't fully grieved. These can accumulate. Inside we are sad about so many things. You can write grief letters about a lot of things that you have lost. Or even more, be sad about them. Cry, reflect, spend time with them. Then let them go.

Journal Prompt 3

Everyone has their different ways of experiencing anger. Some suppress it, some quickly "express" it. How do you typically express your anger? How do you feel after you express it (or withhold it)? How might you do it earlier? How might you express it in a respectful way? I notice that when I am angry that I need to sleep on it. It sits in my body for a long time until I can rest. The next day I can think more clearly about the situation and decide on the best path forward. How do you think you best can deal with situations that make you angry? What might be your own anger process?

Journal Prompt 4

We all have needs. Some are physical, many are relational (best met with others), and some are personal. What do you need? How often do you need them to be met? How might you best meet those needs? Remember you are responsible for getting your own needs met, no one else is. Others can help you but if you don't know what they are and then don't understand them well, then it is very difficult to meet them. Other ideas: Looking back, what advice would I give to myself in high school? Who are 5 people I admire?

Journal Prompt 5

What are my best qualities as a friend? Make a list. What is my superpower? What habits do I have that don't help my growth mindset? What is the kindest thing I have ever done for someone else?

Journal Prompt 6

When is your self esteem most precarious? Why? Is it being alone? If so, how might you start building new friends? Is it reminders of your ex? How might you remove them from your life, at least temporarily? Or minimize your time with him/her?

Journal Prompt 7

Loving ourselves is hard. It is easy to devalue our health, our time, our money, etc. Reflect on how you might love yourself better? If what you say, do, and think matters then how might you change how you interact with others? If you love yourself, how would you know? Often loving ourselves also requires self compassion. Being kind to ourselves is awkward for some. How can you speak to yourself with compassion? The mirror exercise: take 5 minutes and look at yourself in the mirror. Just keep looking. What do you see? What do you feel inside? What do you see in yourself that is beautiful? Your eyes? Your mouth? What makes you unique? Many people find that they fall in love with themselves when they do this. What is your experience? Other ideas: What would I most like to change in the world? Why is my safe person my safe person? How can I improve my communication with the people I love?

Journal Prompt 8

For many people, communication is a very weak muscle. It feels awkward to listen to someone that is upset and not take it personally, or want to help or fix it. How have you handled difficult situations in the past? What is your "go to" method for handling conflict? What do you think about the 4 step communication process (NVC)? Write out a situation with conflict in your life and go through the 4 step process for yourself. What do you observe about yourself? What do you feel inside? What do you need? What is your request? Other ideas: What do I look for in a friend? What form of communication works best for me? How do I communicate that?

Journal Prompt 9

Think back on your former relationship. Now that you have new insight into relationships write down what you want to do differently going forward. Also, what are areas where you need to practice being in a relationship?

Acknowledgments

We would like to acknowledge the vulnerability and courage of the thousands of people we have worked with over the years. It takes a unique person to be willing to dig deep and do the self exploration required to Rebuild a life after heartbreak. We value the people that have contributed to this book, whether directly or indirectly.The world has serious challenges and divorce can be a pattern that carries from generation to generation. By dealing with root causes people that "do the work" are breaking that cycle. We honor you for making the world a better place.

We would like to extend our heartfelt thanks to Margaret Lambert of PuffinsPresentations.com for her invaluable contribution to this workbook. Margaret's decades of experience in running the Rebuilding Seminar program since the late 1990s have provided her with deep insight into the healing process. Her development of the "Marriage Autopsy" questions has been instrumental in offering meaningful guidance to those going through divorce recovery. We are deeply grateful for her generosity in allowing us to include these questions, and her commitment to providing resources that help individuals heal is immeasurable.

About the Authors

Nick Meima is a divorcee and a widower. He has been providing individual coaching and a facilitator for the 10-Week Rebuilders program since 2011.
He has: a Bachelors in psychology
Masters in Marriage, Family, & Child Counseling, MFT
Masters in Gerontology, MSG
8 years of spiritual and psychological counseling training
1 year of training in group facilitation
20 years seeing clients in private practice

Kevin Van Liere is a certified Life Coach and a Rebuilders Divorce Coach. He has worked with people dealing with heartbreak individually and in group sessions since 2018. Using his two divorces as his catalyst for self improvement he has since worked with thousands of people. (He also has two boys that are absolutely amazing.)

Thank you for sharing your time and energy with us!